Hidden City

Adventures and Explorations in Dublin

KARL WHITNEY

PENGUIN
IRELAND

PENGUIN IRELAND

Published by the Penguin Group
Penguin Ireland, 25 St Stephen's Green, Dublin 2, Ireland
(a division of Penguin Books Ltd)
Penguin Books Ltd, 80 Strand, London WC2R ORL, England
Penguin Group (USA) Inc., 375 Hudson Street, New York, New York 10014, USA
Penguin Group (Australia), 707 Collins Street, Melbourne, Victoria 3008, Australia
(a division of Pearson Australia Group Pty Ltd)
Penguin Group (Canada), 90 Eglinton Avenue East, Suite 700, Toronto, Ontario, Canada M4P 2Y3
(a division of Pearson Penguin Canada Inc.)
Penguin Books India Pvt Ltd, 11 Community Centre, Panchsheel Park, New Delhi – 110 017, India
Penguin Group (NZ), 67 Apollo Drive, Rosedale, Auckland 0632, New Zealand
(a division of Pearson New Zealand Ltd)
Penguin Books (South Africa) (Pty) Ltd, Block D, Rosebank Office Park,
181 Jan Smuts Avenue, Parktown North, Gauteng 2193, South Africa

Penguin Books Ltd, Registered Offices: 80 Strand, London WC2R ORL, England

www.penguin.com

First published 2014
001

Copyright © Karl Whitney, 2014

The moral right of the author has been asserted

Set in 13.5/16 pt Garamond MT Std
Typeset by Jouve (UK), Milton Keynes
Printed in Great Britain by Clays Ltd, St Ives plc

A CIP catalogue record for this book is available from the British Library

ISBN: 978-1-844-88312-7

www.greenpenguin.co.uk

MIX
Paper from
responsible sources
FSC
www.fsc.org   FSC™ C018179

Penguin Books is committed to a sustainable
future for our business, our readers and our planet.
This book is made from Forest Stewardship
Council™ certified paper.

For Laura

Contents

1. Broken City   1

2. On the Edge of the Edge   15

3. The Hidden Rivers of the Liberties   38

4. 'James Joyce lived here'   64

5. To the Lighthouse   99

6. Down the Drain: On the
   Trail of the City's Sewage   116

7. The Bus Game   142

8. Ghosts of the New Wild West   174

9. Ballsbridge, Ghost Town   200

10. Suburban Decay   213

11. Flight Path   233

12. On Reaching the Liffey   244

Acknowledgements   263

1. Broken City

Dublin disappeared behind me as I pedalled up Stocking Lane, an old road that leads from the suburb of Bally-boden into the foothills that rise south of the city. The roar of six lanes of traffic on the M50 motorway was quickly muffled by the hedgerows and trees that thickened around me, and I was alone with the bike.

I'm not a good climber. As the incline grew more severe and my progress slowed, I began to notice, or imagine, mechanical problems. The click of my chain echoed off the boundary walls of the houses adjoining the empty road. The rear tyre was dragging slightly.

I was ascending what are universally known as the Dublin Mountains. In truth, none of the slopes within the county boundary is more than a foothill, and even the contiguous Wicklow Mountains contain no peak higher than a thousand metres above sea level. But while the Dublin hills aren't particularly lofty, they loom large above the mostly flat cityscape.

I had been up Stocking Lane before, but I had never attempted this climb at the end of such a long cycle: on the day in question, I had already covered about sixty kilometres. My energy levels were dropping. I hoped the muesli bar, dark chocolate and energy gel that I had eaten while standing in a car park next to Rathfarnham Castle – my white and blue bike propped against an ivy-streaked stone wall – would be enough to get me through to the viewing point at Killakee, below which the city unfurls like a tatty rug. I fetched a bottle from the holder attached to the bike's frame and drank some barely diluted blackcurrant squash.

By this point I had reason to question the wisdom of my day's itinerary. The idea was to cycle across the city from north to south, the journey culminating in the panorama visible from Killakee; but this had involved crossing the city twice, because I had set off from my home in the southern suburbs. Also, for the purpose of the exercise I had defined the city broadly: extending from Swords, a substantial town in its own right but very much a part of greater Dublin at its northern extreme, to Killakee, well south of the point where dense suburbs give way to rural foothills. I hoped thus to test the continuity of a city that I had long viewed as broken into barely connected fragments, a place where the urban, the suburban and the rural interacted in unexpected ways. When I thought of Dublin, the city where I'd lived for most of my life, I thought of edgeland housing adjoining lonely link roads, smashed glass in supermarket car parks, the trickle of a pungent river as it passes through a concrete pipe below a dual carriageway, mobile-phone masts disguised as trees on high ground. It was, it had always seemed to me, a city defined more by its margins than by its centre, and more by its hidden places than by its obvious landmarks.

A cyclist in red Lycra came into view a few hundred metres ahead of me. He, too, was ascending, and pedalling quickly, having dropped into a low gear. I presumed that I would soon pass him. But then I looked down to see my own feet spinning wildly: my gear was as low as his; we were travelling at the same speed. There was no chance of overtaking him, and I now merely wished to keep him in sight as a way of maintaining my pace.

I passed the entrance to the grounds of the Hell Fire Club on Montpelier Hill, built as a hunting lodge around 1725 by William Conolly, a one-time speaker of the Irish Houses of Parliament, and subsequently used by the eponymous club as a meeting place. The club was formed by a group of Protestant noblemen in around 1735, and included among its members Richard Parsons, the 1st Earl of Rosse, a libertine and freemason, and Henry Barry, the 4th Baron Barry of Santry, who was, aged twenty-eight, tried and convicted of murder by a jury of his peers. (Barry was sentenced to death, but was later pardoned.) A painting of the club's interior by James Worsdale shows Barry and a number of other members seated around a table dressed in velvet coats and wearing powdered wigs; behind them, an arched window opens on to a romantic landscape of roiling skies against which silhouettes of trees can be glimpsed. Rumours of hauntings and satanism persist in accounts of the building, along with suggestions of cat sacrifice and a reputed instance of cannibalism. The building is visible on its hillside from across south Dublin, but I had never visited it until a few years before my cycle journey, when some friends and I climbed up to it via the forest trails. Constructed in the Palladian style, the clubhouse has an extremely rough outer appearance and resembles a robust but disused church. The stone walls form an empty shell; the wooden floors are long gone. A storm once blew the roof from the building, an incident attributed by some to the devil. I pictured Satan, dressed in red Lycra, belching fire across the roof before climbing on his bike to resume taunting any lone cyclists who were struggling up the hill.

I put my head down, watching fractions of kilometres slowly click away on the LCD screen of my odometer. At this stage, it was all I could do to keep some sort of focus – watch the distance covered and count the houses. Once I reached the gate of one called Granite Villa, travelling by now at walking pace, I knew that I was nearly at the viewing point.

When I arrived at the top of the hill – tired, faint, dehydrated – the world opened up to me again. I got off the bike, rested it against the waist-high granite wall. I looked down at where I had come from. The city of Dublin stared blankly back, as if daring me to find the right words to describe it.

On the main street in Swords, the notional starting point, I'd edged my bike through sluggish traffic, cutting into a narrow space between a bus and a truck before almost being knocked down by a distracted motorist who failed to see me. I was wearing a bright-green cycling top and a purple neckwarmer, and the frames of my sunglasses were an aggravatingly electric shade of yellow; I was pretty sure I'd stand out, but I was wrong. As the car shuddered to a halt across my path, I pulled the brakes and my rear wheel slid from under me, before righting itself as I pedalled on, having changed direction slightly to get around the car's bonnet. A couple of hundred metres on, the same thing happened again, but I was better prepared. Life for cyclists on the roads of central Dublin has improved somewhat in recent years, but in Swords the car is still the unchallenged king, and I felt myself an interloper.

Swords is an old settlement that feels very new. The crenellated battlements of Swords Castle, which was built in around the year 1200 for the first Anglo-Norman Archbishop of Dublin, face straight down the main street, which is lined on either side with small shops, restaurants and pubs. Further along, there's an outdoor shopping precinct, and further still, a large shopping mall surrounded by a car park. To the west of the town is an extensive area of housing built between the 1970s and the present day. According to the census of 2011, Swords is the eighth-largest urban area in Ireland by population, with 36,924 people – larger than Kilkenny or Navan – and it is in the new estates that most of those people live.

Forest Road, which I followed out from Swords and towards the airport, is – like many roads on the edges of

Dublin – a combination of winding country lane and busy suburban highway. Every so often, a stretch of overgrown cycle lane would come into view on the pathway next to me, often terminating near an ill-defined patch of grass or beside a high kerb. At one point, slightly intimidated by the roaring traffic behind me, I moved to the cycle path, only to find that it soon rejoined the footpath, pointing me straight at a bus stop at which a mother and child stood. I got back on the road. Soon the houses and apartments were gone, the hedges and trees fell away and a vista opened up: I could see directly across the runways and apron, past parked planes to the airport terminal buildings.

Cycling around the airport gave me a new understanding of the city's topography. North Dublin seems very flat, but the road from Swords to the airport brings you perceptibly uphill. The airport sits on a plateau just high enough to offer a fairly clear view downhill to the city centre. The Dublin Mountains still seemed a very long way away as I stood on my pedals, staring over the fence at an Aer Lingus jet taxiing by.

Rolling across the interchange with the M50 into Ballymun, I encountered the usual confusion about cycle lanes. Exiting a roundabout, I joined a cycle lane which seemed to appear out of nowhere and was reached using a pedestrian crossing. I coasted down the hill, looking to my right, to see the blue and yellow Ikea warehouse surrounded by waste ground just north of Ballymun. The cycle lane was brand new, surfaced in red cinder that left chalky marks on my tyres. I looked more closely at the cycle lane's surface, and saw fragments of glass, pieces of wire and angular chips of black plastic – rubbish that had accumulated on it: the detritus of the modern roadside familiar to cyclists, who are forced to contemplate such flotsam and jetsam closely or else risk a puncture.

When I was a child, our family would go for drives around Dublin – sometimes, during the summer, to the mountains, and sometimes to the airport, which still seemed unaccountably exotic in the late 1980s, and where we would walk to the viewing areas in the terminal building from which we could watch planes taking off and landing. We would often drive home from those airport trips through Ballymun, and I remember how the central shopping area was surrounded on all sides by a bulwark of concrete tower blocks – then a unique sight in Ireland. (From a distance, the towers resembled a circular pagan tomb.) There were seven fifteen-storey towers, each named after one of the leaders of the 1916 Rising, and nineteen eight-storey 'spine blocks', built in the 1960s to supply council housing for Dublin's rising population and to accommodate those cleared from inner-city slums. Over the years, the area acquired a reputation for crime and drug use – ills that were attributed, in some quarters, to high-rise living.

In March 1997, a regeneration of Ballymun was announced. The towers would be knocked down, their residents rehoused in new low-rise apartment buildings and houses; and there would be various schemes for social and economic development.

Arriving in Ballymun from the north, I could immediately see how much had changed, at least physically. In the absence of the towers, the main street felt much more spacious and airy than the canyon I remembered passing through as a child. Oddly, the redevelopment of Ballymun had also seen the construction of a new high-rise building: the Metro Hotel, which I judged to be at least sixteen storeys high and which, like many hotels built during the boom, was perhaps surplus to the requirements of tourists and business travellers. Spotting a child's bike parked on a glass balcony, I wondered how many of the hotel's rooms were rented out to tenants who might otherwise have been housed in council blocks. High-rise living wasn't quite dead in Ballymun.

My rear tyre began to drag: a puncture. At a set of traffic lights, I spent a second cursing my luck, then climbed off and pushed the bike towards a patch of grass outside the low-slung Church of Our Lady of Victories, opened in 1969. The church's undulating roof line had triangular peaks and troughs that brought to mind a mountain range or a financial graph.

I picked up the bike and held the top tube of the frame to flip it over. Then I balanced it on its handlebars and saddle. I unclipped the rear wheel, wobbling it free from the chain, and placed it on the grass. The tyre was completely flat. I rubbed my thumb around its circumference, expecting to come across a piece of glass or, perhaps, wire. I couldn't find anything inside the tyre except a solitary pine needle hanging from the grooved black rubber. I had used these tyres for nearly two years and never before experienced a puncture. It seemed implausible that a pine needle had caused it, but I didn't dwell on the puzzle too long. The tyres were supposedly puncture-proof, but I knew that nothing was unbreakable, and that everything was subject to decay: tyres, buildings, cities, people.

Once the tyre was off, I replaced the burst tube with a spare I had in my backpack. I inflated it with a small pump and was soon on the bike again.

At the pedestrian crossings on O'Connell Street, the lights were green for road traffic. Even so, I had to dodge crowds of pedestrians who crossed in front of me, oblivious of anything that wasn't motorized and noisy. Behind me now was the Spire of Dublin – a 400-foot stainless-steel pin that had been erected in 2003. I rumbled across the Luas tram tracks, then traversed O'Connell Bridge – crossing the Liffey – in the direction of Trinity College. My rear tyre was still a bit soft – the pump in my backpack couldn't inflate it to a high enough pressure – and as a result I was able to feel every bump in the road.

To my left was Trinity College – 'set heavily in the city's ignorance like a dull stone set in a cumbrous ring', Stephen Dedalus thinks, in Joyce's *A Portrait of the Artist as a Young Man.* Dame Street owes its width to the Wide Streets Commission, a group of politicians and businessmen convened by an Act of Parliament in 1757 to establish broad thoroughfares in the city's narrow, crooked medieval streetscape. The grandeur of the street was still evident, even as I cycled past a patchwork of empty shops and fast-food joints that depended on passing trade from drinkers boozily stumbling between the George's Street market area and Temple Bar.

Climbing Cork Hill, I passed City Hall, a spectacular example of neoclassical architecture in which a floor mosaic records Dublin's vaguely threatening city motto – *Obedientia Civium Urbis Felicitas*: Happy the City whose Citizens Obey – against a background of three burning castles. It might be said that, on this basis, Dublin was an unhappy city; but if you wanted to go looking for where it all began – the crucible of Dublin's existence as a settlement – around here is where you should look.

When the Vikings arrived in Dublin, in around the year 841, there was already a Gaelic settlement known as Áth Cliath on the south bank of the Liffey near the current site of Father Mathew Bridge. The Vikings settled close to a small pool that bulged from a sharply angled curve of the River Poddle, on the current site of the gardens of Dublin Castle. The Gaelic *dubh linn* – 'black pool' – was adopted by the Vikings for the name of their settlement Dyflin. The arrival of the Anglo-Normans in 1171 ended the rule of the Vikings, who withdrew to the settlement of Oxmantown on the north side of the river. As settlers came from England and Wales to live in the city, Norman Dublin became increasingly fortified – walls were erected, with gates at entry points to the city. These walls ran from the site of Dublin Castle at the south-east in a north-westerly direction to where Father Mathew Bridge is now, then eastwards along the southern banks of the Liffey to the mouth of the Poddle. Outside the walls, suburbs developed in the areas known as the Liberties, lands where native Irish had settled.

I was now approaching the Liberties. At St Patrick's Cathedral, I noticed that the doorway of its west front was situated a few feet below street level – a sign of the slow but constant accrual of layers of the city over the years since the church's construction sometime in the thirteenth century. My tyres zipped across the tarmacked surface, the ruins of Dublin's past buried not far below.

When I was twelve, my family moved from Tallaght to Ballyboden; and so, as I cycled through Rathfarnham village and turned up Willbrook Road past the Yellow House pub, I felt I was on home turf. I began to relax – perhaps a little too much.

I passed the stone courthouse to the left of the road and, further on, a housing development built in the grounds of Riversdale House, which was leased by W. B. Yeats from 1932 until his death in 1939. It was a refuge for Yeats, and was portrayed in his poetry as a place of withdrawal from the world, even as he performed his tasks as a senator and entered an association with Eoin O'Duffy's quasi-fascist Blueshirt movement. Years ago, before the grounds were cleared – 'Grounds where plum and cabbage grew', according to Yeats's poem 'What Then?' – I hopped over the wall and walked through the overgrown gardens towards the house, which Yeats had described as 'small' but which was actually a substantial three-bay construction. I stared through the aluminium windows. The house was being used as offices; telephone directories, filing cabinets and dated-looking office furniture filled the rooms. Later, three large detached suburban houses, each almost as big as Riversdale, were built in its grounds.

The road I was cycling along had been built in the early nineteenth century for, according to local historian Michael Fewer, 'a military purpose: the neutralization of the Wicklow wilderness as a place of asylum for rebels and bandits'. I thought back to a walk I had taken along the same road some years before. On a quiet night not long after heavy rain had begun to work its way down the mountain through pools, streams and rivulets, I heard the unusually mighty rumbling of the narrow Owendoher River, which runs alongside the road. The river's roar reminded me that corn, paper and threshing mills had once, in the eighteenth and early nineteenth centuries, harnessed its power along the banks between Rockbrook and Rathfarnham villages, making the stretch along the Owendoher one of the earliest parts of County Dublin to become industrialized. The remnants of some of these mills could still be seen here and there, their empty stone husks reminders of a long-vanished past.

I turned the final corner and pedalled towards the viewing point at Killakee. It is marked by a row of trees and a stone wall and, sometimes, on sunny days, an ice-cream van will pull up beside the car park across the road. I climbed from the bike, sat on the wall and drank what little liquid was left in the bottle I'd filled a few hours before.

When cities grow, they tend to expand laterally at their margins and vertically in the centre, but Dublin's growth has been almost exclusively of the first kind. The recent boom pressed the city into green fields on the urban periphery but barely affected the city-centre skyline, and in this it was in keeping with long-established patterns of expansion. In the nineteenth century, the development of red-brick suburbs drew richer residents away from their homes in the inner city, leaving a yawning chasm of poverty in Dublin's centre: grand Georgian houses, built for the bourgeoisie, were subdivided for tenement use. Later, many of these decaying tenements – which had provided suitable conditions for the spread of diseases such as tuberculosis and cholera – were knocked down as part of a programme of slum clearance, and in the first half of the twentieth century vast new working-class housing developments were built on the fringes of the city: Crumlin, Cabra, Marino. These new estates – consisting mainly of low-density, semi-detached family homes – established a blueprint for later suburbs, including the one where my parents bought their first house, in the 1970s.

From the viewing point, I could see the green hills I had cycled through give way to the streets of the suburbs, which grew denser as they reached north towards the green-domed church at Rathmines. Tallaght was obscured by the mass of Montpelier Hill to the west, but otherwise I was looking at a near-complete panorama of greater Dublin. To the north-east, edging into the Irish Sea, was the Hill of Howth, south of which, at the centre of Dublin Bay, were the two chimneys of the Poolbeg power station, beside which the mouth of the Liffey tapered into the city before disappearing amongst the clutter of buildings in the centre. Beyond the power station I could see the hulk of Lambay Island, off the north Dublin coast. Newer buildings were generally more visible than old ones: the white of the Luas bridge at Dundrum, the spaceship-like Aviva Stadium at Lansdowne Road and the hulking Convention Centre along the quays. Looking out across all of this, I considered the project I was about to undertake: a series of journeys and forays in search of the city's secret places and untold stories. I intended to haunt the vast suburban housing estates, the waste ground between buildings, the sewers and underground rivers. I wanted to talk with people who knew these locations well and who could tell me more about the things that had happened there in the distant or recent past. I hoped to make a portrait of the edges of Dublin, the hidden city.

2. On the Edge of the Edge

On a frosty morning in late November, I set out from my parents' house to walk around the edges of Tallaght.

I cannot be entirely objective about Tallaght. I lived the first twelve years of my life there; its houses and back gardens and driveways and roads are the stuff of my earliest memories. Its popular image – a troublesome, working-class, crime-riddled suburb-city in the hills – is very clear. What is less clear, even to a native, is its basic geography. A journey around its circumference would, I hoped, allow me to capture a sense of Tallaght as a distinct place – or, perhaps, confirm its essential indistinctness.

Tallaght is an ancient village turned sprawling modern exurb divided from the inner Dublin suburbs by the asphalted canyon of the M50. It has no formal geographical boundary. Ireland's electoral system attributes thirteen electoral divisions to Tallaght: Avonbeg, Belgard, Fettercairn, Glenview, Jobstown, Killinarden, Kilnamanagh, Kiltipper, Kingswood, Millbrook, Old Bawn, Springfield and Tymon. Thus Tallaght could be defined as the territory covered by those thirteen contiguous districts. However, such a definition would exclude other areas that are commonly considered part of Tallaght; and it would include places to the west that are generally considered to be outside it. I had my own idea of what was Tallaght and what was not, and so before I left the house I hastily sketched a map on a sheet of A4. Its borders included trajectories along straightish lines following the boundaries of Kiltipper Road to the south and Tymon Lane to the east. Other boundaries were harder to define. Where, for example, does Tallaght end and Saggart, a village to the west, begin? In any case, I drew my lines, and the route of my walk followed them, with only the odd diversion.

Tallaght was one of the four rural villages to the west of Dublin that were designated in the 1960s for development as new towns to accommodate the city's growing population. The others were Clondalkin, Lucan and Blanchardstown. It was anticipated that each of these new towns would grow in a straight line westward, separated from one another by green belts providing parkland for leisure. The initial plans for the new towns, set out in Myles Wright's 'Dublin Region' report of 1967, envisaged the provision of amenities within a well-designed urban structure – shops, churches and schools were to be sited centrally in small, walkable, town centres. Wright's new towns were to be based around the car: he dismissed trains as unattractive and peripheral bus services as economically unviable. He argued that rising prosperity would make mass car ownership possible, and that the car should form the basis of the state's transportation policy. Wright envisaged that Tallaght's population would eventually grow to around 100,000. He was not far off: between 1961 and 1981, Tallaght expanded from a rural village of 4,565 inhabitants into a sprawling settlement with a population of 56,608 in the thirteen electoral divisions. Once the new housing estates had been built and occupied, Tallaght's development slowed significantly: by 1991, the population had increased to 62,785, and it had reached 71,481 by 2011.

The new town grew up around the nucleus of a very old village. In the eighth century, a monastery was founded by St Maelruain a short distance to the east of the present-day town centre. Although the monastery was raided by Vikings in AD 811, it continued to function until after the Anglo-Norman invasion of Ireland in 1169, when Tallaght became the property of the Diocese of Dublin. In 1310, the bailiffs of Tallaght received a royal grant to enclose the town as a defensive measure against hostile incursions from the O'Byrne and O'Toole clans; no trace remains of these original defensive walls. Further fortifications followed, with Tallaght Castle being built around 1324, just to the east of the monastery site. The castle was largely demolished in 1729 by the archbishop, who built a palace on the site, preserving only a tower from the original building. By 1821, the palace had fallen into disrepair and was replaced with Tallaght House, which was purchased in 1855 by the Dominican order. The new priory buildings also incorporated the preserved tower from Tallaght Castle.

In the nineteenth century, a few mills were built in the vicinity, mainly along the fast-flowing River Dodder, a mile to the south of the main street; but it seems that Tallaght remained mostly agricultural until the twentieth century, when Urney's chocolate factory opened on a former RAF airfield on Belgard Road, a little north of the village. In the land around the village, there were big houses – many of them farms – on which stood remnants of fortified houses and castles. Some of these structures, built to repel native Irish clans who conducted raids from their bases in the forests and hills to the south, were still standing when the new housing estates were being built. Many were demolished; others at least partially survive. One photo taken on the Kilnamanagh estate in the early 1970s shows Kilnamanagh Castle just before it was pulled down: a whitewashed three-storey stone structure with a pitched roof, thick walls and a few very small windows, overlooked by a row of white-painted semi-detached homes of the sort that I grew up in.

According to the plan I had made, Kiltipper Road marked the southern boundary of Tallaght, and so I started at its junction with Old Bawn Road, from which it curves uphill in a south-westerly direction for around a mile before following a broadly straight line from east to west for another mile. The older housing estates I passed as I walked its length were made up of semi-detached houses; the newer ones comprised clusters of apartment buildings. There's a point on the hill where the estates abruptly end, and the remainder of the road, the second mile of Kiltipper Road, running from east to west, is a country lane, used by vehicles taking short cuts at high speed.

I edged through some undergrowth into a clearing, where I sat down and admired the view while muffled hip-hop bled from cars rushing by just a few feet behind me. Extending down the slope below me, between the trees lining Kiltipper Road and the vast swathe of housing that stretches from Killinarden northwards, was a ribbon of green I'd never seen before – a fairly substantial expanse of grassland, some of which was used by motorcyclists, judging by the muddy circuit that had been traced across one field. Adjoining this field were two football pitches, one full-sized and laid on grass, the other a smaller, all-weather pitch. Both were surrounded by floodlights set on tall columns. The open fields contrasted strongly with the density of the social housing beyond – the estates of Killinarden and Jobstown, built to accommodate thousands of people who had been on waiting lists for council housing.

I walked westward until, about three kilometres from my starting point, I went straight through the junction at which Kiltipper Road ends and becomes Kiltalown Lane. In the yard of an old farm, I saw a recovery truck parked next to a grey delivery van which was stripped of its wheels. In front of the van was a pile of four wheels which could well have belonged to it, and other wheels were scattered around nearby. Further along Kiltalown Lane I watched a stream's slow-moving water merge with domestic rubbish that oozed from refuse bags,

combining to brew a dull, thick sludge. Near the end of
the lane, there was an explosion of rubbish: old duvets
rolled up, bound tightly with string, cast into the hedgerow; the wheel of a car; a perfectly fine-looking television,
resting awkwardly, upturned, on one of its corners; endless
discarded carpets; whole beds, upside down, alongside
matching mattresses. It was like a post-apocalyptic ver-
sion of the Argos catalogue. Along a barbed-wire fence
next to a red metal gate, two mud-caked household mats
had been hung out, apparently to dry.

No traffic passed as I walked along Kiltalown Lane.
This was presumably explained by the series of orange
warning signs I had noticed: first 'Kiltalown Lane Closed',
then 'Construction Traffic Only', then 'Road Closed', followed by 'Site Entrance 50m Ahead'. I reached the site
entrance, which formed a dead end – the red metal gate
spanned the road, making it impassable. An orange sign
that hung on the gate read 'No Through Road'. Still
another sign told me that the area behind the gate was
the property of South Dublin County Council, and a
final one warned me of security patrols. Above me, on
the ridge of the hill, silhouetted by the weak winter sun,
was what looked like a concrete wall.

I later found out that this construction was going to
be a reservoir, part of a new network to supply the
ever-escalating demand for water in the south and west
of Dublin. The contractor hired by the council for the
job had gone into receivership a few weeks before I
arrived there and bits of equipment lay strewn inside the

gate: a diesel generator set on a chassis of four car wheels; unidentifiable bits of twisted metal; and wire fences bent out of shape. The building site was deathly silent: work had ceased indefinitely. In the shadow of the reservoir, there was evidence that someone had tried to set fire to the scattered piles of rubbish: the charred remnants were mixed with mud, making it difficult to discern where the road ended and the countryside began.

If it had been possible to continue along Kiltalown Lane, I would have been able to trace the very outer edges of this part of Tallaght, but instead I retraced my steps to the junction I had passed a few minutes earlier and turned left on to Killinarden Road. It was a minor detour, and one which didn't pull me too far off my intended trajectory. I walked downhill between hedgerows that line a rural landscape interrupted only by large electricity pylons, before reaching a modern private housing estate at the foot of the hill. Beyond it I crossed a muddy field rutted with tyre tracks; it was overlooked by several blocks of small two-storey houses, built in terraces of four and each painted a different colour: yellow, white, red, green. This was the western side of the Killinarden estate, built for council tenants in the early 1980s. Nearby, a pink building housed a grocery store; it was set slightly apart from a row of residential houses and its walls on both storeys were covered in graffiti in a variety of colours ('Pato W. is fat') and grubby daubings where earlier graffiti had been painted over.

The juxtaposition of the huddled housing of Killinarden with the open hills seemed to me to encapsulate many of the problems that result when housing is constructed on the very edge of a city. The location isn't by any means unpleasant, but there is an unavoidable feeling of isolation, and I could easily see how one could feel stranded here.

I continued north, crossing the dual carriageway into Jobstown, whose terraces of houses appeared almost identical to those in Killinarden. Having walked westward along Fortunestown Road, I turned north-east along Jobstown Road, passing a number of three-storey apartment blocks that were interspersed with terraces of two-storey houses. Although some of its housing was very similar to the type I had seen in Killinarden, Jobstown had to some degree overcome its atmosphere of isolation through westward expansion: new private housing estates and apartment developments had been built, and its proximity to industrial estates at Citywest brought some jobs and a passing trade for shops and pubs.

At the junction with Fortunestown Way I turned right, heading north-west past newer, red-brick housing: two-storey houses, built in terraces of four. A pub from which extended a church-like clocktower was the most salient feature of the next roundabout; I turned north-east again, along Brookfield Road, passing a Travellers' halting site which was located a few metres from the road, beyond a strip of untidily overgrown green space. Across from the halting site was Brookfield Youth and Community Centre, a recent addition to the area: its grey paint scheme was offset by colourful rectangular panels and red metal letters that spelled out the name of the centre along its north-west façade. I had reached a wide link road, a dual carriageway that cut through western Tallaght, connecting it with motorways and other western suburbs. It struck me that some of the broad, linear open spaces that I had known when I was a child had actually been land reserved for roads such as this – these scrubby lands had been far more interesting to us than the blank spaces designated for 'amenity'. It seems to me now that the threat of their domestication hung over them and added to their sense of possibility. I remember seeing from Greenhills Road the canyon-like waste ground that adjoined the estate in which I had lived; I can recall later cycling along the same ground, on which the earth had been compacted in preparation for the M50 motorway, wondering what it would look like in the future. At the community centre, I looked to the north. Beyond a tall concrete wall I could see a grassy mound of earth and hear the noise of machinery: this was the site of a large quarry run by the Roadstone company. On the northern horizon huge grey silos emerged from behind the terraces of houses.

I crossed the dual carriageway, walked south-east for around two hundred metres, then turned left into the Fettercairn estate, which lies north of Jobstown and runs along the southern boundary of the quarry. This was the northern edge of Tallaght: the rows of houses give way to quarries and woodland. I continued on, past the building occupied by the Fettercairn Youth Horse Project – a local initiative that aims to enable young people to develop expertise in animal care. While I was growing up, it was common to see horses in fields and even back gardens in west Tallaght; sometimes horses ran free. This phenomenon – which could also be observed in other urban and suburban settings in Ireland – led to the introduction of the Control of Horses Act in 1996, which required the stabling of horses, something that was financially impossible for many horse owners. Nevertheless, a love of horses persists in west Tallaght, and the Youth Horse Project seeks to channel this into practical skills. Several horses trotted freely around a small outdoor arena that was set back a little from the road.

I had intended to carry on eastwards from here, past the Belgard housing estate and into Kingswood and Kilnamanagh, in the process continuing to follow the northern boundary as defined by the quarry. But it was now the afternoon and I hadn't eaten. My energy levels were falling and I began to feel dizzy. Facing a choice between going on with the journey as planned or diverting towards the shops, I chose to divert. I mentally redrew my plan: I would head east towards the shops around the Square shopping centre, then north towards Kilnamanagh, before rejoining the eastern boundary of Tallaght, along Tymon Lane. Together with the pangs of hunger, I felt a slight twinge of guilt: getting food entailed abandoning the line I had drawn across the north of Tallaght.

In Aldi, my low blood sugar brought me straight to the confectionery aisle to pick up two packets of jelly beans and a six-pack of Titan bars. I stepped out of the shop, ate a couple of bars and felt a little better as my system began to absorb the sugar. I looked at the empty office buildings next to Aldi, a couple of which had never been completed – the glass façade of one was short several panels, leaving a gaping hole that exposed concrete floors and steel girders.

I walked towards Belgard Road, following it north to the disused Jacob's biscuit factory, then east past Airton Road's many industrial units, before reaching Greenhills Road. Here I was on familiar territory – I was nearing Kilnamanagh.

In September 1972, an article in the *Irish Times* reported on plans for a 1,500-house 'garden town' at Kilnamanagh. It gave the address of the development as Greenhills Road, Walkinstown, and a spokesman for its developers, Tom Brennan and Joe McGowan, said that the new estate would provide 'the ideal environment for modern living'. The estate, which would house seven thousand people, was located, the article asserted, 'in rolling countryside'. An artist's impression showed sizeable semi-detached two-storey family homes amply shaded by mature trees, while abstract figures clad in bell-bottoms responsibly tended to their children in neatly trimmed front gardens.

Kilnamanagh promised to be a bucolic escape from the decaying inner city. My parents, who were living in a rented flat above a shop in Crumlin village at the time, both worked in industrial estates to the north of Tallaght: my father as a buyer with the supermarket Quinnsworth and my mother as a receptionist at the headquarters of McInerney's builders. Houses in Kilnamanagh were sold from the blueprint: on seeing the showhouse, my parents bought the house that would be built on the site next door. Once it was habitable, they moved in, although the road outside wasn't yet finished. There were no houses at the rear, there was a farm down the road and there were still open fields near the estate.

My brother was born in 1975, and I was born three years later. Kilnamanagh expanded, covering the fields with seemingly endless streets and a wide central reservation of smoothed green space that was used for playing pitches. A shopping centre was built – the first in Tallaght – bringing significant traffic into the estate, and the area of land south of the estate came to be increasingly industrialized. My mother told me that, although she liked the place at first, as the development of the area accelerated she found it to be increasingly oppressive.

In, I think, 1984, word got around that a group of Travellers, recently displaced by the construction of the Tallaght bypass – a dual carriageway that traverses Tallaght roughly east to west – was about to set up camp elsewhere. A gang of Kilnamanagh residents, fearing an influx, took turns watching the entrances to our estate. People sat out there all night. They used oil barrels with a panel cut away so the hot coals could be stoked as makeshift stoves for heat. I was five or six, too young to register anything but the general unease of that time, but I later learned from talking to my parents that they had been genuinely scared. Anyone who refused to side with this group of residents was threatened with violence: if they didn't change their opinion, their front windows would be *put in*.

The memory of the oil barrels burning through the night came back to me as I walked past a small strip of land adjoining Greenhills Road used as a park. This park abuts the entrance to Kilnamanagh. Now neat and verdant, it was once waste ground surrounded by mounds of earth put there by locals to discourage Traveller encampments. I used to climb over those heaps of earth, taking a short cut to the bus stop. At one stage I rode my BMX over them. They were perfect for stunts and, although I wasn't big enough or skilled enough to do complicated stunts effectively, a simple climb up one side of an earthen pile and down the other was enough to fire my imagination.

For a while I believed that the accepted idea of 'landscape' – the kind of thing you'd see in paintings and read about in poems – was alien to my experience. That was in part a function of where I was from: the flat, green spaces between housing estates didn't feel any more natural or look any more picturesque than the roads they adjoined. Streams were channelled underground, and when they did surface they smelled strongly of chemicals.

Nevertheless, my primary school class regularly ventured out on nature walks, often to the grounds of the Dominican priory across the road. I returned from one of these walks with a twig from which oozed a strange fungus. I placed it on the nature table that we maintained at the back of the classroom. As it sat there I began to imagine it oozing spores and primeval goo, and became convinced that its presence was making me sick.

I didn't hate Tallaght, but I knew it wasn't like the towns and cities I saw on TV or read about in books. The subjects I studied at school – geography, history, literature – all seemed to refer to places unlike the place I was from. Although I had never looked down on Tallaght – I don't remember ever wishing that I lived anywhere else – there was a certain jaundiced pessimism in the way I viewed the place, one that lifted only years later, after I had moved away. By that point, I could see that 'landscape' was, in fact, all around me, and, if I looked hard enough, an industrial estate could be more interesting than a meadow.

Walking past the estate at Kilnamanagh, I turned in the direction of Tymon Lane, a narrow road that runs between hedgerows from the back of the Cuckoo's Nest pub on Greenhills Road, through a public park, past the side of the National Basketball Stadium, as far as the junction with the old Tallaght road. Beyond this, a path leads you under the messy confluence of the motorway and the Tallaght bypass, past the weir on the River Dodder that was built to channel a flow of drinking water to the River Poddle. I would follow this little road through Knocklyon and onward to my parents' house in Ballyboden. Tymon Lane dates back to the Middle Ages, when it linked a number of castles along this defensive boundary of Dublin city. As I walked, I could hear the leathery rumble of tyres on the M50. Tymon Lane had changed over the years – in appearance, in function. But I took some encouragement from its dogged persistence in a place where so much else had been erased.

Some time after I had completed my circumnavigation of Tallaght's boundaries, Tomás Maher, a local historian, agreed to show me around what remains of the old village. We met at a café in the offices of South Dublin County Council and decided to head to St Maelruain's Church for a look around the cemetery and perhaps to gain access to the church building.

St Maelruain's, a Protestant church built around 1820, stands on the site of the eighth-century monastery with which, as far as we know, the settlement of Tallaght began. The church integrates into its structure a medieval turreted bell tower that was part of an earlier building; the A-shaped outline of the pitched roof of the previous church is visible on the tower's stonework. Now, all around the site was movement and modernity: boxy buildings and noisy buses. I found it difficult to visualize the monks' lives of quiet contemplation.

There was no answer at the sexton's cottage, but eventually we located her husband, who showed us the inside of the church. Then he handed us a set of keys, encouraged us to push them back through the letterbox of his house when we were done and sent us off to climb the bell tower.

I heard a throaty squawk coming from the trees in the graveyard and looked up to see a heron perched awkwardly on a branch. I had been told by the sexton's husband, and by Tomás, that herons in the area had become almost tame, taking food from people in the parks. I recalled the awe with which I regarded herons when, on family holidays in West Cork, we glimpsed them standing in the low tide. At that time they kept their distance and had an air of wildness about them, but now, in Tallaght, they were often to be seen on the roofs of houses. I couldn't help but feel that some of their aloof charm had been lost.

Climbing up the bell tower, we passed through a series of stone chambers, one above the other, linked by a narrow spiral stone staircase. When we reached the top, the sky opened up above us. An iron bell, dating from 1890, hung from two modern girders that were beginning to rust. I clambered uneasily up some steps to a turret at the corner of the tower and, clinging to the wall for safety, viewed Tallaght from above for the first time in my life.

From the bell tower, my first impression was that this busy modern place had once again become a small rural village. Behind a tall stone wall, the thick trees of the priory grounds obscured the unfinished apartment blocks near the dual carriageway. The old police station and the sexton's cottage contributed to the atmosphere, and for long stretches no vehicular traffic passed by, this section of the road having been reserved for buses. I could see the curve of the Old Blessington road, which skirted the grounds of the church and along which the steam-tram had once run. To the south, I could see the straight line of the Old Bawn road leading uphill in the direction of the lower slopes of the mountains, to Killakee and the Hell Fire Club. Below us, rendered tiny by the height we had attained, people picked their way around the graveyard. The heron took flight in the direction of the tall trees of the nearby Dominican priory.

However, my first impression soon proved untenable. Beyond the police station was a four-storey red-brick office building built in the 1990s, and, when I turned to the left, I could see the boxy white and silver industrial buildings along Belgard Road. Stretching from the church towards the west was the graveyard, which was itself now surrounded by white buildings several storeys tall. What I saw when I looked west from the bell tower was Tallaght's industrial and commercial centre.

I thought about what happens when you leave a place, but it does not leave you.

My family left Tallaght a few weeks before I finished primary school, so for those weeks I commuted from our new home in Ballyboden, a largely middle-class suburb a few kilometres east. The dislocation that resulted from this commute made me feel as though I were straddling two completely different worlds.

Tallaght was where I had lived my whole life up until then: it was where I had walked a mile or so to school up Greenhills Road, where I had sung in the church choir in the Dominican priory, where I had cycled my bike and kicked my football around on the street in front of our house. In the Tallaght I had grown up in, there was a mix of middle-class and working-class families that made the place enjoyably unpretentious, but there was also a desire to educate and improve oneself that could be seen in many local initiatives: creative-writing courses; the community radio station that ran from a cottage on Greenhills Road and on which my mother presented a weekly show; and the Tallaght Boys Choir, which during my time there was run by Father Tom McCarthy, an ambitious choirmaster who frequently secured radio appearances for us and, memorably, a few performances on the stage of the Gaiety Theatre as street urchins in *Carmen* and *Tosca*.

Although Ballyboden wasn't so far away, it felt very different: the accents were different, the way people viewed themselves was different. It felt as though I had to start again. People had a confidence, an expectation of success, a calm sense that you were entitled to everything you had and held, that I hadn't really seen before. The longer I lived in this new area, the more Tallaght felt like the flipside of middle-class Dublin, a cautionary example. Tallaght was working class; Tallaght was tough;

Tallaght was violent; Tallaght had thousands of houses and very few buses; Tallaght had Travellers; Tallaght had vigilantes who didn't want Travellers living near them; Tallaght was a place you wouldn't ever go near unless you actually lived there: the Wild West.

We had moved, but we were still from Tallaght, as my cousin and I were reminded one day when we were kicking a football about on the road. One of our neighbours, a middle-aged man whom I had never met before, confronted us, saying that people from Tallaght should stay away from his house. We were quiet and unassuming children and didn't really know what his problem was – and my cousin was from Drogheda!

I soon learned that if you wanted to blend in with the Irish middle class, you had to pretend you were from nowhere. Following the example of your neighbours, your schoolmates or your fellow workers, you had to assume a kind of middle-ground identity similar to the one they exhibited. At my new secondary school, any sign of what would traditionally be thought of as a working-class Dublin accent – such as difficulty pronouncing the letter *h* or a thickening of the *d* or *t* in certain words – would be mocked by other students. I should add that my brother and I didn't quite share these pronunciations – we were the children of parents who were both from outside Dublin. Thus, in principle, we had much in common with the middle-class south Dubliners who policed accent in this way, many of whom were first-generation Dubliners whose parents distrusted any sign of Dublin identity. Perhaps it should have been easy for me to embrace a certain kind of blandness, a flatter mode of speech, but I found it difficult. Was I from Tallaght, and if so should I act like I was from there? I thought about how someone from Tallaght would act. I hadn't considered it before, and now I found it difficult to define myself.

Ballyboden and the suburbs around it, Knocklyon and Rathfarnham, had grown gradually, the new estates taking on some of the characteristics of the older ones.* Tallaght, in contrast, had grown quickly, the recently built estates sprawling across formerly agricultural land. Lacking an established identity, it became a melting pot of working-class Dubliners, middle-class families in starter homes and peripatetic Travellers. Working-class life was changing – people were being encouraged to buy houses and cars, to plan for the future, to expect things to get better – and Tallaght became a staging

---

* This kind of respectability by proxy was illustrated when developers lobbied to gerrymander postal codes so that estates on the border between codes would be placed in the more desirable area. The property developer Seamus Ross told the Mahon Tribunal in 1996 he had paid the politician Liam Lawlor £40,000 to get the postal address of a new housing estate changed from Clondalkin, Dublin 20, to Lucan, Co. Dublin. In the mid-1980s, the Irish postal service proposed that the postcode of Dublin 6 should be split in two – Templeogue, Kimmage and Terenure would become Dublin 26, while Rathmines and Ranelagh would retain the Dublin 6 code. Residents whose postcode would be changed objected, complaining that it would devalue their property, and eventually An Post relented. The new postcode became Dublin 6W – Dublin 6 West.

ground for identities. Ballyboden, on the other hand, was rule bound: people were – or anyway seemed – solidly middle class, and very few cracks showed in their patina of respectability.

The move from primary to secondary school proved to be a difficult one for me. By the time I was fifteen years old, I had stopped going to school altogether.

After I had completed my primary schooling in Tallaght, I was sent to a private secondary school housed in an old stately home that surveyed the city from the side of a mountain. It was a couple of miles from our new house, and was like nothing I had ever experienced. My brother had already been attending for some years, making the journey between our house in Tallaght via a number of different buses. My parents, thinking this school suited my brother, assumed it would be good for me, too. I knew that at this school students were ranked according to the grades they got, and would receive a monthly report printed on a pink sheet of paper that told them where they stood. This felt odd and made me anxious.

What had no doubt seemed colourful and delightful features to parents when they visited on open days became to me threatening symbols of oppression – the rugged stone walls and tree-fringed playing fields; the oars fixed to the walls of the hallways which hinted at what, as far as I could tell, was a completely fictitious heritage in the sport of rowing. The school was run by

Opus Dei, a sect that, to a degree I didn't fully grasp at the time, sat at the extreme end of Catholicism. The priest-to-student ratio seemed strangely high, while the headmaster and at least one of the teachers were lay members of the institution. In Tallaght, I had sung in the church choir, gone to Communion and Confirmation like almost all of my classmates in our Catholic-run state school. Catholic practice and belief was part of my weekly routine. Yet at this new private school they advocated an airless belief system I found alien. The school's distance from the city – even from the nearest suburb – made me feel imprisoned, locked out from the world that you could glimpse beyond the lower hills. Weekly Masses were held in a small chapel inside the main house, and this reinforced my feeling of isolation. At my primary school in Tallaght, any time we spent in a church was in the priory across the road, where members of the public came and went as we gathered for Mass or confession.

Beside the entrance to the school was a whitewashed cottage in which lived George Reid, a man in his late sixties who used often to greet passers-by, including students of the school whose bus left from a stop adjacent to his house. On a cold, wet morning just before Christmas in 1992 he was found dead in the school grounds, in a pool a little way upriver. A few students were selected to represent the school at the funeral, which was held in the church next to the Yellow House pub in Rathfarnham. During the service, I sat on the cool wooden bench and felt a chill. The school crest on my navy-coloured, V-necked woollen jumper showed a blue stream flowing between two red hills. On the crest was a motto that read, in Latin: 'The river will always find a way through the mountains.'

Just over a year later, in January 1994, a few days after returning from Christmas holidays, I quit the school and never went back. I had spent my whole life on the edge of the city, and now it felt as though I were in danger of falling off.

I was diagnosed with depression. My parents, shocked at having a son who seemed to have given up on life so completely, asked me to see a therapist who operated from a large bungalow in a south Dublin suburb overlooking the sea, not far from the railway line. And that's how I found myself travelling through the city just after rush hour one morning a week.

I remember the freedom I felt at being able to roam through central Dublin on bright spring mornings. I remember wondering at the tatty grandeur of Pearse station as stray beams of sunlight cut through its dusty, cracked windows. I remember, when travelling on the train, the way the view of the bay opened up after the station at Sydney Parade, and how I could see across to Howth Head, the blue of the sky reflected in the bay. At a time when I felt cornered, these glimpses of the city held out faint shards of hope for a future I couldn't yet imagine.

3. The Hidden Rivers of the Liberties

'Right leg in there, left leg in there. Right arm in there, left arm in there.'

I was standing beside an open manhole on Werburgh Street, around the corner from Christ Church Cathedral. I was preparing for a descent into the underground tunnels that conduct the River Poddle beneath the streets of Dublin and eventually into the Liffey at a point along the south quays. The plan was to walk upstream, towards the Liberties, a district to the south-west of the city centre whose evolution over the centuries had been shaped by a network of rivers that are now hidden underground. I had already put on a white suit made of paper to protect my clothes from anything I might encounter in the tunnel. I was wearing a red safety helmet and clear plastic glasses to stop my eyes getting splashed. Now I stepped into a harness that would catch me if I slipped while descending the ladder.

Two white vans were parked by the kerb. Four men in the high-visibility clothing of Dublin City Council's Drainage Services division stood near the open manhole, from which an aluminium ladder protruded. There were two additional men, who wore the same kind of paper suit I was wearing: Robert Buckle, the council's

Area Engineer, and Dave Greene, who also worked for the drainage division. Dave had earlier urged me, in what I thought was an almost mystic manner, to just 'enjoy the journey'. I took it to be his way of telling me that I shouldn't worry about being trapped underground.

After the harness was secured, a gas mask was clipped to my belt. If we encountered breathing difficulties – caused by a gas leak, for example – I was to take the mask from its case and put it over my nose and mouth. We also carried a gas alarm, which tweeted every few seconds to tell us everything was okay. If it went berserk, we were in trouble.

Dave and Robert climbed down the ladder, and I watched as a cable, which was connected to a tripod that stood above the manhole, was attached to their harnesses. Then they were gone, below the street, and it was my turn.

I stood facing the ladder, felt the cable being clipped to my back and put my foot on the first rung. I was wearing thigh-length wading boots which I had been handed in the Drainage Services stores earlier. They were three sizes too large, and my feet slipped slightly as I climbed down.

Suddenly everything was dark. I could hear Dave's voice telling me how far it was until I'd reach the river bed. 'Ten feet, Karl . . . five feet . . .'

I stepped off the final rung on to a bank of silt next to the base of the ladder. Dave pointed his torch at the ground – clear water a couple of inches deep ran all around where we stood.

The base of the tunnel was broad and flat. An arched cement ceiling supported the city above us.

We walked eastward, towards a point below Dublin Castle's Ship Street gate. The cement ceiling gave way to stone; then, after we stepped through a narrow aperture where the water momentarily became noticeably deeper and flowed faster, the tunnel widened to a barrel-vaulted red brick. We ducked under a rusting iron sewage pipe that cut straight across the tunnel.

When we reached the area below the Ship Street gate, there was a sharp drop in the ceiling, bringing it down from a height of about twelve feet to around three. We could continue in that direction if we crawled, but instead we turned around and walked south-west towards St Patrick's Cathedral. I watched a Lion Bar wrapper float gently by. This was the first piece of rubbish I'd noticed in the river, although later I saw a white bucket bobbing along.

We passed the entrance to a red-brick tunnel that led off to the left. The tunnel was full of rubble, bricks and empty glass bottles, and no one really knew where it went.

Robert stopped dead in his tracks and turned to Dave.

'Who's Noel Ryan?' Robert said.

Dave said: 'Who's who? Noel Ryan?'

'Did you ever hear of him? He came in here one night and sprayed his name on the wall.'

Robert turned his torch towards the wall, where Noel Ryan's name was written in yellow paint.

As we walked, the main sound was the sloshing of our boots through the water – it echoed around the tunnels. The water reached just above my ankles, and flowed slowly. Dave reached down and swept his gloved hand across the surface, cupping some of the water in the palm of his hand to show me how clean it was.

Now we were in what Dave told me were the oldest sections of the tunnel. Blocks of stone were cemented in place and weathered planks of dark wood showed through the cement, a reminder, he said, that the tunnels had originally been constructed from wood. This section of the Poddle had first been tunnelled in the seventeenth century.

We reached a long, straight tunnel with low concrete walls and a vaulted brick ceiling that had been constructed when the road above was widened in the late 1980s – a significant modernization of this section of the Poddle tunnel. Directly above us was Patrick Street, a busy four-lane road that runs the short distance between the city's two cathedrals, St Patrick's and Christ Church.

As we walked, I became aware of a patch of light ahead of us: a ladder, bathed in daylight from an open manhole. Once we had safely been lowered into the tunnel at Werburgh Street, the council workers had driven to this point to help us back out. From the darkness beyond the ladder – towards the point where, at street level, Patrick Street meets Upper Kevin Street – I could hear the sound of rushing water. It sounded like a waterfall.

None of us wanted to leave the Poddle. Not yet, anyway.

'Ah sure, we'll walk up to it,' Robert said, and we continued around the ladder and deeper into the tunnels. Earlier Dave had talked about what he called 'the boxes' – a pair of pre-cast concrete tunnels that channelled the Poddle under the crossroads at St Patrick's Cathedral from the direction of Blackpitts in the Liberties. The tunnel curved right, and we followed it. Ahead of us were the boxes: two rectangular tunnels that were each perhaps three feet tall and twelve feet wide. They sat a foot or so above the level of the tunnel we stood in, creating a ledge from which the water fell – the sound of rushing water that we had heard as we stood near the ladder. In comparison to the barrel vaulting of the brick tunnels we had earlier passed through, the boxes seemed functional and grim: 'Just to show you that modern engineering has no soul,' Robert told me.

We turned back from the boxes and, before returning to the ladder, Dave and I ducked down a narrow, low-ceilinged stone tunnel. Robert stayed behind in the main tunnel in the dark – Dave and I had taken the only two torches with us. The tunnel we were in connected to the sewer system: if there was a blockage in the sewers, the overflow would be directed into the Poddle and eventually into the Liffey. The end opened into a red-brick chamber in which three sewer flows met: one coming west from the Coombe, another south from Clanbrassil Street and the third from the direction of

Kevin Street. In contrast to the generally clear water of the Poddle, the sewage was a murky brown. We turned back towards the main tunnel, where we met Robert, standing in the dark.

'When you went away with the torches, Davey, it's pitch black here,' Robert said.

'Sorry, Robert,' Dave said.

'No, no,' Robert said, to indicate it wasn't a problem.

'There's no light getting in at all?' I asked.

'You can't see your hands in front of your face, like,' Robert said.

We walked towards the ladder and, once the safety cord was lowered down and attached to each of us in turn, we climbed up to the surface and emerged through the open manhole on the pavement in front of St Patrick's Cathedral.

Over a year prior to climbing into the Poddle and walking between Werburgh Street and St Patrick's Cathedral, I had walked around the Liberties in the company of Franc Myles, an archaeologist who had carried out numerous excavations in the area. Franc told me about an occasion when, in order to trace the path of the Commons Water, one of the underground rivers that flow through the Liberties, he had to go underground himself. He and a fellow archaeologist, Steve McGlade, had been excavating a site at the north-west corner of the junction of Ardee Street and Cork Street, below which the stream ran, and where he and I were standing when he told me about it. 'We said "Fuck it," you know? "We're archaeologists, we can't just let it run under the building and not investigate it," so we did.' Franc and Steve climbed into the culvert that channelled the stream below Ardee Street and walked east, in the direction of St Patrick's Cathedral. The barrel-vaulted brick culvert was big enough for the two archaeologists to walk in if they crouched slightly. They waded through a constant flow of water of about a foot in depth. 'We got as far as the far pavement' – here Franc gestured towards the kerb on the opposite side of the street.

As the archaeologists edged through the culvert, Franc observed three separate manholes overhead; they had probably once led to now-demolished buildings, and had since been sealed with sandstone slabs. Fifteen metres east of the building they had been excavating, they noticed an abrupt step-like drop, of about a foot, in the limestone-slab-lined floor of the tunnel. Franc suspected, from having looked at old maps and leases, that this was the point at which the stream in which he and Steve were wading – the Commons Water – met another water-course, the Abbey Stream. In nature, when rivers meet, they merge; but in the highly engineered netherworld of the Liberties, these two watercourses cross paths in their respective culverts and continue on their separate ways. Although the archaeologists couldn't see the Abbey Stream – it was hidden in a culvert above them, which was indicated by a slight drop in the ceiling height of their tunnel – they were sure this was where it crossed above the Commons Water.

These and other watercourses were once central to life in the Liberties. Over the centuries, they were diverted to provide drinking water, to supply breweries and to power mills. The natural boundaries they created were also used in dividing one administrative area from another. In the absence of proper sewage systems, however, the rivers became polluted conduits for disease. By the end of the nineteenth century, they had been covered over and mostly forgotten.

However, even though they're hidden from view, it's still possible to walk their paths. Once you're properly attuned, a dip in the road can be enough to tell you that a river runs below.

The Commons Water rises in Drimnagh, a couple of kilometres south-west of the Liberties. The Abbey Stream is a man-made watercourse redirected from the most substantial of the streams that cross the Liberties, the River Poddle.

The Poddle rises in Tallaght, near Cookstown, and flows through Templeogue, where it was once joined by a volume of water fed from a weir on the River Dodder at Balrothery. Next to a small housing estate in Kimmage, a tongue-shaped masonry take-off known as the Stone Boat redirected a portion of the Poddle water into the City Watercourse, which ran in a north-westerly direction, parallel to Sundrive Road, then by Rutland Avenue into Dolphin's Barn; it provided fresh water to Dublin city for hundreds of years. Further north, near the present-day entrance to Mount Jerome cemetery, the monks of the Abbey of St Thomas created the diversion known as the Abbey Stream. The function of this new stream was twofold: to demarcate the western boundary of the monks' lands, and to provide them with their own supply of fast-flowing fresh water. Initially, the water was used to power mills and to drink; later it supplied breweries and tanneries in the area. The original course of the Poddle had marked a shared boundary – the landowners on the eastern side of the river could use the water too. (Perhaps this explains why, when choosing a course for the artificial diversion, the monks placed it slightly inside the western boundary: this water wasn't for sharing.)

Both the Poddle and the Abbey Stream are channelled separately under the Grand Canal. While the main course of the Poddle flows below the Liberties street known as Blackpitts, near the eastern flank of the area, the Abbey Stream flows under the National Boxing Stadium on South Circular Road and emerges briefly at the entrance to an industrial estate on Donore Avenue, before continuing north to Marrowbone Lane. From there, it loops eastwards before doubling back and passing above the point where the two archaeologists had stood, then travels parallel to Mill Street before rejoining the main course of the Poddle at the end of Blackpitts, flowing along New Row towards St Patrick's Cathedral. At Donore Avenue, another branch, known as the Tenter Water – which follows the course of the older Hangman's Stream – channels some of the Abbey Stream water directly to Blackpitts. (A few years ago, an underground car park in one of the apartment buildings near where the Abbey Stream is reunited with the Poddle was flooded by the overflowing watercourses, and cars were submerged in the pool of river water until the inundation subsided.)

The Poddle reaches St Patrick's Cathedral and flows south through the tunnel that I walked along with Dave Greene and Robert Buckle, turning eastwards along the old wood-lined tunnel under Ross Road before flowing into the grounds of Dublin Castle beneath the Ship Street gate. The river subsequently curves around the site of Dublin Castle, flows under the Olympia Theatre and empties into the River Liffey through a grating on the south quay between the Millennium footbridge and Grattan Bridge. In the 'Wandering Rocks' section of *Ulysses*, Joyce writes that 'from its sluice in Wood quay wall under Tom Devan's office Poddle river hung out in fealty a tongue of liquid sewage'. (In fact, the Poddle emerges at Wellington Quay, but Joyce scholars maintain the mistake was intentional.)

The Poddle has also been known as the Pottle, the Puddle, the Salach and, further upstream near Tallaght, the Tymon. The Commons Water, being a wholly separate river until it joins the Poddle at the end of the Coombe, is an innocent bystander in all of this. Yet its course, which crosses the artificial diversions of the Poddle, ensures it is often mistaken for the better-known river. When walking along the courses of the rivers, I frequently had to remind myself which one I was standing above, and which one I was about to intersect.

I was born in the Liberties, in the then new Coombe hospital on Cork Street; and during my childhood in Tallaght we passed through the area when taking the number 77 bus into the city centre. I remember the tightly packed red-brick streets as a vivid contrast to the windswept housing estate where my family lived. I was always intrigued by the sharp turns the bus took at the junction of Cork Street and Ardee Street, and then again from Ardee Street into the Coombe – I didn't know, then, that every street in this part of the Liberties follows a river. During the medieval period, this S-shaped arrangement of streets was known as the Crooked Staff. Cork Street runs west to east alongside the Commons Water, while Ardee Street runs north to south above the course of the Abbey Stream, and the Coombe follows the course of the Commons Water towards where it joins the Poddle.

Today 'the Liberties' is a single district of the city, but the Liberties of Dublin are plural for a reason: there were four of them, originally created in the twelfth century. A liberty was an administrative division of the

Lordship of Ireland, and until the nineteenth century each liberty was independent of the authority of Dublin Corporation. All of the Dublin liberties – Thomas Court and Donore; St Sepulchre; Christ Church; and St Patrick's – had their origins in charters granted to religious orders. Thomas Court consisted of the lands surrounding a large Augustinian monastery. After the Reformation and Henry VIII's dissolution of the monasteries, the liberty was granted to the Brabazons, Earls of Meath. The liberty of Donore was also added to their estate – thus Kenneth Milne, in *The Dublin Liberties, 1600–1850*, refers to 'Thomas Court and Donore' as a single liberty. In the Liberties, even a single liberty could be plural.

In my twenties, I lived for about four years in the Liberties, first in a new apartment block not far from Meath Street, and then in a red-brick nineteenth-century terraced house off Blackpitts. I didn't realize it, but when I thought of 'the Liberties', I was mostly thinking of Thomas Court and Donore. The apartment I lived in had been outside the liberty of Thomas Court, looking in; the red-brick house had been inside the liberty of Donore, looking out. The house would have had a good view of the Poddle from its front windows, were that river not channelled below the tarmacked surface of Blackpitts.

It was a bright, breezy morning in mid-September when I met Franc Myles at a café on the South Circular Road. We planned to walk around the boundaries of the liberty of Thomas Court and Donore and, at the same time, trace the paths of the underground rivers. Franc explained the logic of the excursion: 'What fascinates me as an archaeologist is the sense of difference and the sense of place. How different was your life ten metres inside the liberty or ten metres outside the liberty, or was there a difference at all?'

Franc is six foot five and in his late forties, with greying hair gelled straight up in spikes. On the day in question, he was wearing a bright-yellow high-visibility vest with the word 'Archaeologist' printed on it in black letters and a pair of streamlined Ray-Ban sunglasses; he wore both the vest and sunglasses throughout our walk, and pushed a bike alongside him.

He described his main area of research as the 'archaeology of the contemporary past'. He has personal connections to the locality: his aunt lived in Weavers' Square, close to the path of the Abbey Stream; his father worked in the Guinness factory at St James's Gate, through which the Liberties' ancient boundaries run. Franc himself grew up in Kilmainham, not too far from the outer boundary of the Liberties, and lived for a while just off Blackpitts. The pace of urban redevelopment in the Liberties, coupled with the historical interest of the district, has ensured that a large amount of archaeological work has been carried out in recent years, much of it by Franc. Things had grown much quieter by the time we met; in the aftermath of Ireland's economic crash, construction had all but ceased in the area. New apartment blocks were interspersed with sites that had been cleared in the expectation of further building. If the recent past was visible in the unevenness of development in the area, the more distant past was accessible through a subtle reading of the urban landscape.

The arrangement of streets in the Liberties preserves the geographical features of earlier eras in the most unexpected of ways. Leaving the café and turning a corner, Franc gestured east down Greenville Avenue – a quiet street lined on one side by pairs of semi-detached, pebble-dashed houses – towards where it took a severe hairpin bend. On a map, you can see that sharp corners and an unusually jagged layout characterize a series of streets that run from the south end of Blackpitts in an east–west direction: Greenville Avenue, Merton Park, the west end of Merton Avenue and finally Donore Avenue. This irregular arrangement of streets, Franc told me, reflects a line of fortification that dates back to the Renaissance era. The curve he pointed towards would have been a vantage point extending from the fortification wall 'to give a field of fire in every direction'. On the 1837 first edition Ordnance Survey map, he told me, you could see 'a zigzag laneway from the bottom of Blackpitts to Roper's Rest'. Roper's Rest was a house or tavern near the South Circular Road end of what's now Donore Avenue.

On reaching Blackpitts, Franc explained that we were approaching the edge of the liberty of Donore; across the invisible Poddle was the archbishop's liberty of St Sepulchre. Blackpitts follows the original course of

the Poddle and sits in a just-perceptible depression running from south to north through the landscape. Maps
from the sixteenth and seventeenth centuries show the
river flowing along the east side of the road, but it was
subsequently covered over – by the mid-seventeenth century, Franc thinks. There was slight incline towards
Clanbrassil Street to the right, while, to our left, on noticeably raised ground, stood a terrace of five red-brick houses.
I pointed out my old house, and Franc told me that
before these houses were built in the late nineteenth
century there had been an orchard on the site. Further
north along Blackpitts the fortifications we were tracing
had crossed over the Poddle and continued eastwards.

As we walked, Franc referred to his recollections of
various old maps of Dublin, particularly the 25-inch
Ordnance Survey map of 1912, which had been central
to structuring his understanding of the evolution of the
area. Continuing along Blackpitts, he drew attention to a
ruined chimney stack that adjoined another building,
telling me that it was a remnant of a gable-fronted house
in the 'Dutch Billy' style once prevalent in Dublin, and
especially in the Liberties, but now virtually obliterated
from the city's streets.

'The 25-inch map was surveyed around here in 1912,'
he said. 'If you can imagine what the chimney stack
would look like on a map, it'd look like a building with a
sort of a V-shaped protrusion. So what you're effectively
looking at here is a blank space where they've knocked
down the house but they've had to keep the chimney

stack, which is integral to the structure of the other building. So this is a good way of looking, when you look at the 25-inch map: see how many blank spaces there are with these sort of Vs sticking out, and that can give you a good idea of how many Dutch Billy houses there were.'

We strolled towards Newmarket, pausing to look at the redeveloped site of an old distillery that had once drawn water from the Poddle. There had been a facility in the basement for taking water from the river; Franc had once got a look at it – 'I just climbed in, really' – but hadn't had a camera to document what he found.

The terrain of the Liberties is mostly flat, but Newmarket sits on a plateau-like expanse at a slight elevation above the surrounding streets. To the north-east of Newmarket, surrounded by waste ground and, on its northern side, a tall fence, is St Luke's, a Protestant church built between 1715 and 1716 and now severely derelict. In 1975, it closed to public worship, and the building was damaged by a fire in 1986. It now stands roofless, its bell-cote empty – its bell having been moved to St Patrick's Cathedral for safe keeping – while its windows are filled in with concrete blocks and its grounds overgrown and inaccessible to the public.

In 1674, a royal patent was granted for a twice-weekly agricultural market at Newmarket, and construction began the following year. The marketplace was modelled on that of Smithfield, across the Liffey, and a plan for the site stipulated wide approach streets; sheep pens were to line Ward's Hill, at the eastern end of the market site. Water from the Abbey Stream supplied individual properties around the market – including tanneries and breweries – for which property owners paid twice-yearly rates to the Earl of Meath.

During the nineteenth and twentieth centuries, Newmarket underwent a decline in fortunes. The silk trade, which had been fostered in the Liberties since the seventeenth century by Huguenot migrants, disappeared from the area in the nineteenth, while the breweries that had grown up around the rivers didn't last much longer: mass consumption of beer meant that larger brewers such as Guinness thrived while the smaller breweries along the Poddle closed. Watkins' brewery at Newmarket dated from the early eighteenth century; in 1904, it merged with Jameson, Pim & Co., and by 1937 went into voluntary liquidation. This decline was reflected in the fate of Newmarket's architecture. In 1954, the architectural historian and conservationist Maurice Craig wrote that Newmarket was 'no longer of any architectural character'. More recently, the architectural historian Christine Casey noted that 'extensive rebuilding in the mid-1990s has if anything worsened matters'. Nevertheless, perhaps because of its location and vastness – and in spite of its relative disuse – Newmarket is a striking urban space. Franc listed some of the uses buildings around Newmarket were now put to: an evangelical church, a food co-op and flea market, a taxi company, a business manufacturing Indian sauces. Most obvious were the large sheds on the south side of the square with CCTV cameras at each doorway: warehouses used by a multi-national data-storage company.

We stood beside a pub, long closed, at the corner of Brabazon Row and Newmarket. There was a murder here a number of years ago; subsequently the pub had closed, and remained shut. Dull pebble-dash covered the upper level of the two-storey building. 'This thing was a gabled structure originally, and when I got inside it, there were very thick walls, old brick. You can actually see behind the render – see the windows? And when you look at it over here, there is an element of a gable there. Believe it or not, there's a seventeenth-century building here. You'll have to use your imagination.' I narrowed my eyes and looked up, and a series of large square indentations, the former windows, were visible on what would have been a third storey. I pictured a three-storey, gable-fronted building, in brick or plaster, instead of a squat public house. A sign advertised 'beers and good food'. I imagined a damp, musty smell and a long-muffled act of violence. We moved on.

Just around the corner from Newmarket, we stood in a yard that belongs to Dublin City Council. Franc had said that if we walked up a concrete ramp towards a low wall at the rear of the yard we would glimpse the Abbey Stream below us, but the water had been channelled through pipes and covered over so that all you could see was a rectangular stretch of waste ground surrounded by high walls. A council worker told us that the owner of a neighbouring property had taken it into his hands to bury the stream, and that 'a case was being taken' by the council. As we stood in silence, a black and white cat gingerly picked its way along the top of the wall across from us.

We walked down Chamber Street, where a row of elaborate Dutch Billy houses had once stood, then took a brief detour: along Weavers' Square and down a narrow laneway to a little street called Cow Parlour, now surrounded by recent housing developments. (According to Clair Sweeney's *The Rivers of Dublin*, the name comes from the monastery of Conelan, which was corrupted to 'Cowbelan', then 'Cowparlour'.) In the laneway, stone cobbles poke from under a ragged carpet of eroding tarmacadam. Once you notice this, it isn't so difficult to imagine how the laneway and surrounding area might once have looked.

We doubled back northwards and began to track the Commons Water, along the north side of Cork Street. The river marks the boundary between the liberty of Donore to the south and that of Thomas Court to the north. One way of judging its path is to follow a line of likely-looking manholes down a narrow side street, but for us the trail ended where the river ran under a building. Picking up the river's path again on Ardee Street, Franc drew my attention to an old stone wall that was visible through the front and rear windows of the empty ground-floor retail units of an apartment building.

'See the wall in behind? That is a fucking amazing

wall. It's one of the few we've actually found a reference for – off the top of my head, it's either 1682 or 1692. We found a reference to its construction in one of the Brabazon leases. And it was basically constructed to separate land known as the Artillery Field – which was one of these places that during the disturbances in the 1640s [when the Irish Catholic gentry rose up against the English administration in Ireland] they used as an artillery park – and the brewery of William Cheney. Now William Cheney, it turns out, is an ancestor of the former American vice-president, Dick Cheney. So we wrote to him and said, "Any chance of getting a few quid for a publication?" We didn't receive a response. But William Cheney was the first person we know of to take a lease on this plot. Pretty soon afterwards he had developed a tannery, and just where that building stops, that's where the Commons Water comes through. So the site is divided by the Commons Water as such. So you're now in Thomas Court. Once you cross the far end of that building, you're in Donore.'

On reaching the Coombe, Franc and I began to trace the boundary of the liberty of Thomas Court. This was also the course of the Commons Water, but we broke away from that river at a small lane that leads uphill on to Ash Street. The Thomas Court boundary runs parallel to this street. On reaching Carman's Hall – a lane that connects Francis Street with Meath Street – we could look back down along the boundary line and see that it now cuts through the back gardens of the buildings on Meath Street, before continuing along a narrow lane in the direction of Thomas Street.

The lane was made narrower by the car wedged in the centre of the alleyway. Two men, the car's owners, stood to one side and showed no sign of moving. For a brief moment, the situation felt a little threatening. Franc held his bike above his head and squeezed between the car and the wall. I looked to the left and, unexpectedly, my gaze was met by a horse's quizzical stare: along the lane stood a row of stables. A viscid yellow liquid trickled from below the stable doors, along a drainage trench carved in the centre of the alley, and dripped through an iron grating.

These horses pulled tourist carriages around Dublin's city centre, and, although it was a surprise to encounter them here, this was by no means the most unlikely place one could stumble across equine accommodation in the area: I knew of a tumbledown shack where a horse was kept on a corner near Francis Street. Across from it, I once saw a horse being led down the hallway of an otherwise unremarkable two-storey terraced house. I also knew of a large red-brick house off Clanbrassil Street where the residents kept horses and carts in the rear garden. Once, I walked past it expecting to catch a glimpse of the horses and instead saw a team of armed police pin down a handcuffed man in the centre of the street; all guns were pointed towards him.

On Thomas Street, Franc pointed out what he called a 'dog-leg' – a zigzag inconsistency in the frontages of the buildings that indicates construction on irregularly shaped medieval plots. Here, the dog-leg was visible between the Tesco and the Centra.

We cut down Hanbury Lane, parallel to Thomas Street, heading west. Here, we were tracing the old boundaries of the abbey of Thomas Court. Franc drew my attention to a gap in a row of nineteenth-century red-brick houses that led to some small industrial buildings which he thought suggested the persistence of a right of way: 'Every time I'm in the Registry of Deeds I go looking for the original deed to see how that's actually articulated, that little gap.'

'It wasn't a continuation of the street?' I asked.

'No, no – you're very much within the bounds of the abbey now.'

We turned left along the street named Thomas Court, and left again on to Earl Street South, where railings cordoned off a gate-like entrance to an empty yard that had been overgrown by weeds. A rusting street sign behind the railings indicated that this was the old Meath Market. After the monastery's dissolution, its buildings had been cleared by the Earl of Meath and replaced by a cattle market, a rectangular expanse surrounded by houses and abattoirs where butchers sold meat from their stalls to the public. A visit to the market by a sub-committee of the municipal council in the summer of 1876 was recorded by the *Irish Times*, which declared the 'loathsome' Meath Market to be 'the worst locality visited on the South side of the city' and alleged that not one of its twenty-two dwellings was 'fit for human habitation', partly as a result of overcrowding, but also because of their proximity to 'four or five slaughterhouses'. The newspaper report concluded by suggesting that 'the speedy clearance of this area would effect an improvement than which nothing could be more desirable'. Although much of the stone from the abbey had been taken away by the Brabazons, an archaeological excavation carried out by Claire Walsh in 1997 dug through the modern layers of red brick and limestone to discover medieval and post-medieval remnants – roof slates, window glass, sculpted stone, floor tiles. These finds suggest that a good portion of the Abbey of St Thomas Court is still buried beneath Meath Market. At the time of the excavation, the site was owned by a developer, who subsequently failed to get planning permission; now, as the result of a land swap, it belongs to Dublin City Council.

Franc drew my attention to the building to the left of the railings, a dull, single-storey, pebble-dashed construction: 'The funny thing about this is that it has a concrete floor, and as you walk in, the floor comes up. So . . . '

'There's something there?'

'There's something there. In my line of work you look for little hints and little clues – there's some reason why, when you walk into that building, the floor level rises. So I would imagine they're avoiding pretty heavy-duty masonry walls, which is screaming at me: gatehouse.'

The building was probably going to be cleared and a new building erected. Planning permission had already been granted. Before the demolition, Franc wanted to dig there, to see if he was correct in his hunch about what lay below the site.

Rainsford Street isn't the street it used to be. Approximately two thirds of it is now hidden behind the walls of the Guinness factory at St James's Gate. The abbreviated street begins as a continuation of Hanbury Lane but appears to stop short at an eastern gate of the factory on Crane Street. In fact, Rainsford Street continues beyond the factory gate and emerges, through another gate, at the western edge of the Guinness site, at Grand Canal Place. Through a security fence beside the entrance to the Guinness Storehouse, you can see an old green sign on the wall of a factory building still telling you the name of the road: 'Rainsford Street'. Before the Guinness factory divided it, Rainsford Street used to be a fashionable promenade which led in the direction of the City Basin, a substantial reservoir filled by the City Watercourse. Once, Dubliners strolled around the perimeter of the basin on sunny days; now, it had been filled in and built on: a park to the north, a school to the south, with the red-brick Basin Lane council flats in the middle. At the back of the schoolyard you could see a low stone wall with a squat cement staircase leading down into what had once been the basin.

The City Watercourse, which begins by branching off from the Poddle at the Stone Boat in Kimmage, travelled through the Liberties along a series of raised earthen ramparts known colloquially as 'the back of the pipes'. It had its origins in a command from the Lord Judiciary of Ireland, who on 29 April 1244 told the Dublin Sheriff to improve the city's water supply. In 1931, the City Water-course was channelled into the Grand Canal, and in 1984 it was again diverted, to drain into a large sewer that ran along the canal. Channels were also built from the other rivers – the Poddle, the Abbey Stream and the Commons Water – to handle floodwater overflow.

Franc had told me that, even though they're now dis-used, the City Watercourse's ramparts were still partially visible, and we walked into a 1930s housing estate in hope of seeing them. At a break in the line of houses, beyond the end of a back garden, there was what looked like an overgrown laneway, hemmed in by the boundary walls of the gardens. The houses to the far side of the rampart were sited noticeably higher than were those beside which we were standing, indicating a fairly steep incline. At the end of the street, some waste ground was untidily fenced off. Grass grew between concrete slabs: below this, the old watercourse had run.

We cut down a lane past the Botany Weaving Mill – which used to be the Bethany mill. We reached some old stone bollards, on the other side of which was Cork Street. The path of the Commons Water cut across the lane: this was the edge of the liberty of Thomas Court, and the end of our trip around the rivers and boundaries of the Liberties.

The Liberties are sharply delineated – or were. In the

nineteenth century, they were dissolved as administrative units, and now they persist more as a notion than anything else. But it's still possible to walk the edges of each liberty and to imagine the buildings that once stood where you're standing, and the people who've lived and died only a few footsteps away. Sometimes, on a still and silent evening, you can even hear the water rush beneath your feet as you cross one of the Liberties' long-buried rivers.

Our walk finished at Meath Street, a bustling shopping street lined with butchers' shops, bakeries, pubs and discount stores. Earlier, Franc had told me that, in a church on this street, 'they have the representations of all the saints in Ireland – they're along on either side of you, around halfway up on the left – and there's one suspiciously fresh-faced-looking saint. It's actually the death-mask of Kevin Barry. They couldn't find a representation of St Kevin, so they used Kevin Barry instead.' Kevin Barry was an Irish republican martyr who had been executed, aged eighteen, in 1920. Now, as Franc cycled up the street, he turned in his saddle to remind me to visit the church and see the statue he had described: 'He's the only saint without a beard!'

I went into the church and examined the statues of the saints, but they were all painted white and I couldn't distinguish one from another. Even though I had only recently had the statue and its exact location described to me, I was unable to find it. I could have done with a map.

4. 'James Joyce lived here'

Glengarriff Parade was murky in the dim orange light of Dublin street lamps on an icy January night. At the southern end of the street, the Mater Hospital's glass towers glowed against the dark winter sky.

On the corner where the street meets the North Circular Road, there's a newsagent's shop. A man in a tracksuit and trainers emerged from it and headed northward along the pavement. I walked slowly in the same direction along the opposite pavement. I was looking for a house. I had the chilling impression that I was being followed.

I was tired. I was alone. I had already been walking, on and off, for a few hours. Although I had never experienced any trouble in Dublin's inner city, I felt ill at ease as I walked along Glengarriff Parade.

The man on the opposite side of the street slowed down. It seemed to me that he was slowing to match my own pace. I wondered why he would do this. Perhaps I looked suspicious to him – someone intently studying the house numbers, notebook in hand. By slowing down, he immediately became suspicious to me.

I adjusted my woolly red-and-black-striped scarf and checked that the laces of my battered green canvas shoes were still tied. I carried my notebook, and a digital camera in a black canvas satchel which hung from my shoulder.

The man crossed the street and walked a short distance behind me. He carried on a continual barrage of phlegmy throat-clearing and spitting. I assumed he was on his way to a house on this side of the street, and I crossed to the opposite side – the west, where he had been in the first place – and walked until I reached the house I was seeking. He continued along the opposite side of the street, but slowly and behind me so that I could not see him. When I arrived at the front door of number 32, I fetched a sheet of paper from my pocket. Where I stood was quite dark, so I moved a short distance down the pavement, past the next house, to get closer to the low glow of the street light. On the page, there was a long list of addresses, just over half of them crossed out in blue ink. I focused on one address in particular, which I was about to cross off: 32 Glengarriff Parade, the house to which James Joyce, his parents and his siblings moved in 1901.

This end of Glengarriff Parade consists of terraced, single-storey, nineteenth-century red-brick houses. Behind the houses on this side of the street is the perimeter wall of Mountjoy Prison. Number 32 has a bay window and a couple of stone steps leading up to the front door. I took my notebook from the satchel and began to write down my impressions of the house.

I realized that the man across the street had recrossed, to the side I was now standing on. I continued about my business, trying to give the impression that standing in the gloom on a Dublin street writing in a notebook on a winter's evening was an obvious and rational thing to do – why wouldn't I be there, writing in the dark? As the man drew closer, I studied the page of my notebook intently. I heard a front door open, then turned to see it slam shut. The man had let himself into number 32; evidently, he lived there. The shop he had left and the house he was going to were on the same side of the street, along a relatively short stretch of pavement. Why had he twice crossed the road to the side I was walking on? Could he have crossed, the first time, in hope of finding a neighbour at home? It also seemed a remarkable coincidence that the house I was seeking was his.

Disturbed by these events, I crossed back to the opposite side of the road. The light in the front room of number 32 went on. Then it went off. I felt the odd sensation of being observed. I tucked the notebook in my coat pocket and walked back towards the North Circular Road.

I had set out that day to visit all of James Joyce's addresses in Dublin, in chronological order, and 32 Glengarriff Parade was the thirteenth property on my' list. This was where the young Joyce had begun to write down what he called 'epiphanies': brief sketches of sudden revelations – errors or gestures through which people reveal their true selves. The Joyces left Glengarriff Parade after a year. I turned west along the North Circular in the direction of Phibsborough, where they moved next.

Later, I found out that the house I'd stood outside –
the one that the man in the tracksuit ran into – wasn't the
one the Joyces had lived in at all. In the years after
1901 the houses on the street were renumbered, and the
Joyce house was now number 10.

All of James Joyce's major works are set in Dublin, the
city where he mainly lived between his birth in 1882 and
his departure for Paris in 1904. Joyce's life and work have
become part of the city's official heritage: sanitized, nor-
malized, packaged. In gift shops you'll find his image on
a tea towel, on a poster. For years, Joyce's face was, liter-
ally, common currency: it appeared on the Irish ten-punt
note, juxtaposed with an image of the Dublin Mountains and the curving coast of south Dublin.

Over the years, statues of Joyce have been erected
around the city. There's a bust of him on a stone base on
St Stephen's Green, looking rumpled and old; there's
another of him looking stern, middle aged and priest-like
in the courtyard between two huge concrete buildings in
University College Dublin; and there's a full-body statue
that depicts him wearing a coat that looks a couple of
sizes too big for him, outside the Café Kylemore on
North Earl Street. I'm not aware of any statue of the
young Joyce, even though the writer didn't live in the city
after the age of twenty-two, and never set foot in it after
thirty. Joyce's Dublin was the one he experienced as a
child and young man – the Dublin he fixed for ever in
his writings. During that time, as the financial position

of his father deteriorated, his family lived a peripatetic life, tracing an eccentric path around the city.

According to Vivien Igoe's *James Joyce's Dublin Houses*, Joyce lived at twenty addresses in Dublin; the number includes a few places where he stayed for only a couple of days during two post-emigration visits to the city. The first fourteen of the homes on the list were shared with his family – his father, John Stanislaus Joyce, his mother, May, and his siblings. (The Joyce family had ten surviving children, who appeared in extremely quick succession: James, the eldest, was born in 1882, and the youngest, Mabel, in 1893.) After leaving the family home in Phibsborough in 1904, Joyce lived at three addresses on the south side of Dublin before moving to Paris.

Ulysses tracks the movements of Stephen Dedalus, a young man working as a teacher, and Leopold Bloom, a middle-aged Jewish advertising salesman, around the city on 16 June 1904. I wanted to carry out my journey around the city in a single day, too, but in midwinter rather than midsummer. I chose the middle of January for my odyssey because, more than the warmth of midsummer captured in *Ulysses*, winter seemed to me particularly Joycean. The crepuscular grimness of *Dubliners* and *A Portrait of the Artist as a Young Man* seemed most closely associated with the pessimism one feels in Dublin during the winter months.

I set out first that January morning towards number 41 Brighton Square, in Rathgar, where James Joyce was born on 2 February 1882. On the way, I walked past a pub in Terenure that had recently mounted a plaque indicating that Joyce's mother, May Murray, had been born there. I was already aware of a plaque affixed to a house a couple of miles closer to the city centre, on Clanbrassil Street, noting that Leopold Bloom – a wholly fictional character – had once lived there. It was tempting to think that Joycean Dublin suffered from a needless build-up of plaque.

Brighton Square is not a square nor even a quadrilateral but a triangle of substantial two-storey Victorian red-brick houses surrounding a wedge-shaped park. It looked largely untouched by the twentieth century, let alone the twenty-first, apart from the cars parked along its kerbs. A sign attached to an iron gate informed me that the park, which contains a tennis court and a few benches, was private property and that there was 'No Admittance to General Public'. Between the windows on the first floor of number 41 was a rusting plaque erected on 16 June 1964, paid for by students and staff from Montclair State College in New Jersey. Dr Frederic Young, the head of that college's English department, had visited Joyce's birthplace the previous year. He had expected the location to be marked in some way; but instead, he told a *New York Times* reporter, he was 'much disturbed that there was not the slightest indication of its having had any connection with the great author'. When he returned from his visit to Brighton Square, he told a graduate class, who had been studying *Finnegans*

Wake, about the situation. They proposed that funds be raised to mark the site, and that's how Dr Young found himself carrying a 35-lb bronze plaque on a flight to Dublin. At 4 p.m. on 16 June 1964, Dr Young stood on a kitchen chair in the front garden to deliver a speech to the hundred or so people gathered for the occasion. The idea of celebrating Joyce's novel on Bloomsday each year was still a new one. On 16 June 1954, the fiftieth anniversary of the day depicted in the novel, the newly founded Dublin Joyce Society held a pilgrimage that included among its number the writers Brian O'Nolan, Anthony Cronin and Patrick Kavanagh, who hired two horse-drawn carriages to bring them between locations mentioned in *Ulysses*. On Bloomsday in 1962, the society opened a Joyce museum in the Martello tower in Sandy-cove; and, at the unveiling of the plaque at Brighton Square, Dr Young pointed out that his was only the second Joycean plaque in the city, after the one at Sandy-cove. (A journalist writing about the event in the next day's *Irish Times* pointed out a third: a 'James Joyce lived here' sign was already attached to a house in Blackrock.) The commemoration of Joyce, and in particular Blooms-day, was only getting started.

Brighton Square figures in Molly Bloom's monologue at the end of *Ulysses* as the place where Molly's family, the Tweedys, lived before she married Bloom. While there's no explicit reference to the address in *A Portrait*, in 1931 John Joyce wrote to James asking if he remembered Brighton Square in the days 'when you were baby

Tuckoo, and I used to take you out into the Square and tell you about the moo-cow that used to come down from the mountain and take little boys across'. We have no way of knowing whether John Joyce would have had any such memory himself if he hadn't read the opening of *A Portrait*: 'Once upon a time and a very good time it was there was a moocow coming down along the road and this moocow that was coming down along the road met a nicens little boy named baby tuckoo . . . His father told him that story [. . .] He was baby tuckoo.'

John Stanislaus Joyce was, in the beginning, a man of some means. At the age of twenty-one, he inherited a number of properties in his home county of Cork that had been owned by his deceased father, and he subsequently derived a substantial income annually from them. He also had a solid job: soon after his marriage to May Murray, he was appointed as a collector of rates, at a salary of five hundred pounds a year. Thought of as a sharp wit by his workmates, he was also, in the words of James Joyce's biographer Richard Ellmann, 'inefficient'. When the rates office was taken over by Dublin Corporation in 1891, John Joyce lost his job, aged forty-two. He received a small pension as a result of his wife's entreaties to his former employer. Ellmann describes John Joyce as 'trapped . . . too accustomed to high living to subsist on his low income'. He resented his family, primarily because supporting them entailed spending less on alcohol for himself.

None of this makes it on to the plaque at Brighton Square, nor any of the others that mark Joyce's Dublin addresses, but his family's movements around the city tell a twenty-year story of decline that Joyce was to revisit repeatedly in his fiction. In *Dubliners*, he frequently evokes the atmosphere of the area around Rutland Square – later Parnell Square – near Belvedere College, where he went to school. Two stories in particular refer to streets where the Joyce family lived: North Richmond Street ('Araby') and Hardwicke Street ('The Boarding House'). In *A Portrait* the movements of Stephen Dedalus's family closely shadow those of the Joyces, from the beginning of the book, which depicts a house in Bray that is identical to the one the Joyces inhabited, to the family's move to Blackrock and then the 'sudden flight' from there to the city centre. Joyce subsequently places the Dedaluses at properties which include a semi-detached house at Millbourne Avenue in Drumcondra and a terraced house in Fairview, both of which match addresses the Joyces occupied. When Stephen Dedalus arrives home to Millbourne Avenue, he asks his brothers and sisters, who sit around the kitchen table eating their tea, where his parents have gone. They've gone to look at another house because the landlord of their current property is about to put them out. Stephen also notes that 'a boy named Fallon in Belvedere had often asked him with a silly laugh why they moved so often'. In *Ulysses*, Stephen, who has been living in the Martello tower in Sandycove – as Joyce briefly did – encounters while browsing books on Bedford Row his sister Dilly, who is living with her father and two sisters in destitution, dependent on charitable donations and pawning their possessions. Joyce's brother Stanislaus, in his memoir *My Brother's Keeper*, wrote, 'In Dublin the steps of our rapid downhill progress, amid the clamour of dunning creditors on the doorstep and threatening landlords, were marked by our numerous changes of address.' Each address represented 'a descending step on the ladder of our fortunes', and each particular location was associated in Stanislaus's memory 'with some particular phase of our gypsy-like family life'.

I cut down Brighton Avenue and across the north side of Kenilworth Square, towards Rathmines. As I passed the rugby pitches on the square, I thought of Joyce's jaundiced description in *A Portrait* of the young Stephen Dedalus playing the game at Clongowes Wood College in Kildare: 'He ran after them a little way and then stopped. It was useless to run on.'

On Castlewood Avenue, in Rathmines, I stopped at the next house the Joyces lived in. When they moved there in 1884, John Joyce was – or anyway believed himself to be – on the way up. The house, number 23, is much larger than the one the family had recently vacated, and remains an imposing structure – a three-bay, two-storey red-brick raised over a basement. Steps lead up to the front door, above which is a fanlight. The house barely merits a couple of sentences in Ellmann's book, but the plaque next to the entrance proclaims it to be the place where James Joyce wrote his first words.

*

The Joyces' next stop was Bray, a seaside town south of Dublin. From Rathmines, in 2013, the quickest way to get there by public transport was to take a tram into the city centre and then a train out along the coast. Walking from tram to train, I passed Finn's Hotel, where Joyce's future wife, Nora Barnacle, was working at the time they first met; and I popped into Sweny's Pharmacy, which is no longer a chemist's but operates, staffed by Joyceans in period attire, as a simulacrum of the shop in *Ulysses* where Bloom buys a cake of lemon soap. A man in a white chemist's coat and black dicky bow opened a wooden drawer beneath a glass cabinet that contained many packages wrapped in brown paper tied with string – this, he told me, was how prescriptions were packaged for customers in 1904.

Outside the Royal Irish Academy of Music, I paused to look at the brass plaque on which the name of the organization is embossed, the profile of the letters smoothed down noticeably by years of polishing. I recalled doing two piano exams here when I was a child, and how nervous I was about being assessed in something I felt I had no great talent for. (Joyce, for his part, was a singer of some ability; he took costly lessons at the Dublin Academy of Music, around the corner at Lincoln Place, and won a bronze medal at the 1904 Feis Ceoil, an annual festival of music held in the Antient Concert Rooms.) A woman in a beige trench coat walked up the steps of the academy, as if in a hurry, doing vocal exercises. I turned and, further down the street, I saw a middle-aged man with grey hair slip on a patch of ice and fall face down on to the pavement; the heavy rubber soles of his boots pointed towards me.

The train line from the centre of Dublin to Bray traces the curve of Dublin Bay and then, after cutting through Glenageary and Dalkey, follows a precipitous track along the cliffs above Killiney Bay. According to Stanislaus, with the move to Bray, in 1887, his father hoped, 'as he used to explain politely and frequently, that the train fare would keep his wife's family away'.

The line, which reached Bray in 1854, was built by the Victorian engineer and businessman William Dargan, who also constructed the mile-long esplanade that leads from Bray harbour towards Bray Head, which Joyce described in *Ulysses* as a 'blunt cape' that was like 'the snout of a sleeping whale'. By the time the Joyces moved to the town, it had established itself as not just a fashionable destination for a day out but also a modish residential suburb.

At Daly station, I turned from the platform into a laneway which led through a turnstile on to a road that seemed to tumble downhill towards the seafront. Number 1 Martello Terrace is located as close to the sea as I've ever seen a residential house – it's practically teetering on the harbour wall. It sits at the end of a terrace of eight three-storey houses painted in a variety of colours, overlooked by a Martello tower once owned by Bono.

Between the Joyce house and the sea is a two-storey

boathouse with all its windows blocked up. I walked past the detached boathouse as the seawater lapped over the edge of the harbour, slapping across the stone walkway that leads from the end of the promenade, around the boathouse and behind the houses on Martello Terrace. A yard selling coal and gas was sited overlooking the harbour, just behind the Joyce house. On a stretch of beach between the water and a small car park, some fifteen swans, many seagulls and a great number of pigeons jostled for bread thrown by people who appeared to have come here expressly to feed them. Some of the swans had wandered into the spaces between cars, possibly for shelter from the cold wind.

The plaque affixed to number 1 was straightforward: 'James Joyce Poet-Novelist Lived Here 1887–1891'. While they occupied this house, Joyce's family employed servants, and you can detect them – or fictional representations of them – on the edges of *A Portrait*. At a Christmas dinner in Martello Terrace, the family waits at the table for the servants to bring in 'big dishes covered with their heavy metal covers'. In this scene, Stephen Dedalus's aunt Dante has an argument with Simon Dedalus – the John Joyce father figure – about the fall of Charles Stewart Parnell, the Irish Parliamentary Party leader and tireless advocate for Home Rule who, when named as a co-respondent in a divorce case, was deserted by the Catholic Church and many members of his own party. Writing of the Irish attitude to Parnell in an article for an Italian newspaper, Joyce observed: 'they did not throw him to the English wolves; they tore him to pieces themselves'.

Ellmann writes that 'for John Joyce the fall of Parnell, closely synchronized with a fall in his own fortunes, was the dividing line between the stale present and the good old days'. In the stale present, costs were mounting. These included school fees: in 1888, the young James Joyce was sent as a boarder to Clongowes Wood College.

Sitting on the station platform, I let a train go by while I finished the bag of chips I had bought in a take-away across from the station. On the train, a middle-aged man in a camel-coloured wool coat sat in the seat in front of me. He had stood patiently on the platform, waiting for the train to arrive. It was already past two in the afternoon and I had visited just three of Joyce's twenty addresses. The light was starting to fade, the grey cloud that obscured the weak sun felt oppressive, and my mind felt fatigued. In the chip shop, the television on the wall had been tuned to a station on which a weatherman predicted snow all across Britain. I looked out to sea, towards Wales. In Ireland, no snowflakes fell, but the sky seemed to prom-ise wintry showers at any moment.

The man in the camel coat stayed silent and still until the train began to move, at which point he started to dial numbers on his mobile phone. It soon became clear his business was property. He finished one call, then imme-diately phoned someone else. He called out an email address at which he could be contacted – a firm of solicitors based in Bray – and then made another call. I thought of Leopold Bloom's hustle in *Ulysses* – he spends his whole day working, selling ads, confirming design and space in the newspaper offices, all the while musing internally on past losses and current passions.

At Glenageary station, large blocks of tightly packed graffiti text were spray-painted across the brickwork of the station walls. The words were closely corralled into columns so that from a distance it resembled a medieval manuscript – too closely hewn to be thoroughly legible when seen from any distance. As the train pulled away, I tried to note down some text from amongst the seething scrawl and glimpsed the words 'cancer in my nutsack'.

By 1892, the Joyces had moved to Blackrock. John Joyce had lost his job and had begun to raise money by selling off the property he'd inherited. I got off the train at Blackrock and walked from the station along the main street, recalling a tale Stanislaus Joyce once told about seeing his father on that street, drunk, playing a piano-organ he had seized from the Italian organ-grinder who had been performing there. John Joyce was singing 'The Boys of Wexford' at the top of his voice, while the bemused organ-grinder looked on. Stanislaus, who had been playing down on the foreshore with his friends, passed discreetly on the other side of the street.

I crossed the dual carriageway to the beginning of Carysfort Avenue, seeing as I did so a small white marble plaque, stained by residue over the years, fixed to the side wall of number 23, not far from a battered-looking intruder alarm. It read: 'JAMES JOYCE RESIDENCE restored by T. C. Walsh & Son Limited, 1991'. At the front of number 23, another white marble plaque read: 'in this house lived JAMES JOYCE'. Shortly before the move to Blackrock, James had been taken out of Clongowes and was studying at home, while the other children were sent to a convent school. This arrangement continued at the house in Blackrock. According to Richard Ellmann, James would interrupt his mother's work hourly and ask her to examine him on lessons he had set himself.

A single stone lion stood upright on either side of the front door and another balanced on the roof of the colonnaded portico – an open porch with white pillars on either side. The name of the house, Leoville, was embossed in gold paint on the glass in the fanlight above the door. The front garden was tarmacked, and a small car was parked alongside three wheelie bins.

While I stood there, a queue of traffic began to build up along the road. Perhaps because of my increasingly edgy state, I thought I could detect impatience in each rev made by the engines of the cars, and I didn't feel I could hang around outside the house much longer. I walked to the bus stop outside the Frascati Shopping Centre and caught a bus towards the city.

In doing so, I was following the journey of the Joyces' belongings on the day they left Carysfort Avenue, some time in late 1892 or in the early months of 1893. In

A Portrait, Joyce writes of Stephen Dedalus and his mother being able to see from their railway carriage two yellow caravans bringing their possessions along the Merrion Road from Blackrock to the city centre. Mr Dedalus carries the family portraits with him, as was John Joyce's habit. According to Vivien Igoe, John Joyce 'regarded these as his credentials and they had to be carried by hand'.

I stepped off the bus on the north side of Parnell Square, walked past Findlater's Church and crossed to Hardwicke Street, where Joyce's family spent their first months in the inner city, at number 29. In *A Portrait*, the heart of Dublin is, to Stephen Dedalus, 'a new and complex sensation' compared with 'the comfort and revery' of Blackrock; having timidly explored the area around his new house, Stephen is struck by the 'vastness and strangeness' of the 'bustling life' of the city and its docks. The terraces of Hardwicke Street, like much of this part of the north inner city, were built for the upper classes in the early nineteenth century, but by the time the Joyces arrived the street was shrouded in despair, the once-grand houses divided into tenements. Hardwicke Street is the setting for Joyce's grim story 'The Boarding House', in which a lodger, Mr Doran, tentatively enters into a relationship with Polly, the daughter of the landlady. The story ends with Polly imagining a romantic future, while Mr Doran, his conscience tortured with Catholic guilt, meets her mother to arrange a marriage.

The eponymous house was number 4, at the junction with Frederick Court; it still stands, but the one the Joyces lived in is gone. On the Dublin Civic Survey map of 1925, a number of buildings on Hardwicke Street were marked as 'third class tenements'. In October 1953, an *Irish Times* journalist found a 'ghostly area' with grass sprouting from the basements and steps of the houses, the glass fanlights broken and the windows filled with cement blocks. The people who once lived here had moved, the journalist wrote, to 'the terrifying wilderness of the suburbs, trying desperately to get used to the quiet, the absence of danger from darting vans and hurrying autos'. Most of the Georgian houses were replaced with red-brick council flats in the 1950s. I walked past the entrance to the Vietnamese Irish Association, which is housed in one of the flat complexes, towards the pale stone of St George's Church, with its towering spire. Work on the church had commenced in 1802, around the same time as the surrounding streets were being laid out. Francis Johnson, the architect responsible for the church, lived a short distance away, on Eccles Street – the street where Leopold Bloom lives in *Ulysses*. Johnson at one stage built a bell tower in the rear garden of his home, complete with functioning bells that he frequently rang for his own amusement.

I walked along the line of the street, trying to imagine where number 29 had been. There appeared to be no relationship between the numbers of the flats and the original numbering, and I moved on.

Crossing Mountjoy Square, I saw schoolboys heading home from Belvedere College, the secondary school Joyce began to attend once the family had moved to the north side. I was now walking the route Joyce would have taken from the school to the family's next house. On the east side of the square I crossed in the direction of Croke Park, clearly visible above the roof of James Gill's pub. A broad street slopes downhill towards the North Circular Road – this is Fitzgibbon Street, where the Joyce family moved in early 1893. I stood across the road from the house – which was then number 14 but is now number 34. Three and a half storeys of the building were a dull brown brick, while the top half of the third floor had been rebuilt in a newer, lighter red brick. The house had been divided into flats – six, to judge from the number of buzzers. Through the front window I caught a glimpse of what looked like the white metal handle of a lawnmower. I considered that it could be a buggy, and that I was just trying to see lawnmowers in the most unlikely places. By this time, tiredness was beginning to affect what I saw and how I moved. My legs were feeling heavy. The darkness of evening, which had threatened for much of the winter afternoon, was now beginning to descend. I had seen only six of Joyce's addresses, and still had fourteen to go.

I walked to Dorset Street, past an off-licence where a young, vexed couple were having a loud argument while onlookers avoided looking on. I jumped on a bus for the short trip to Drumcondra.

Millbourne Avenue is a lane running along the wall of St Patrick's teacher-training college. At first it seems too narrow to be anything other than a back lane, but there are a number of businesses – a barber's, a small café, a photocopying shop, a beauty parlour – based in small buildings along the initial stretch of the avenue. Further on, past the rear gates and garage doors of houses backing on to the lane, I reached a row of two-storey terraced houses, among which I found number 2. This was a surprise, because I had read in Vivien Igoe's book that the house had been demolished and replaced with an apartment block. I had also seen, in the same book, a photo that showed a solid-looking semi-detached two-storey house with a front garden surrounded by iron railings. (James's brother Stanislaus, in *My Brother's Keeper*, calls this house a 'small, semi-detached villa in Drumcondra' before noting, darkly, that 'it was at Millbourne [Avenue] that my father made a vague attempt to strangle my mother'.) Thus I was fairly sure that the terraced house on Millbourne Avenue that now bore the number 2 wasn't Joyce's house at all. Regardless, I took a photo of it. Parents were picking up their children from the school in the grounds of St Patrick's, and had parked along the street. Further along the lane, I saw a modern red-brick two-storey apartment block set off from the road and not too much taller than the houses that adjoined it. I fetched Igoe's book from my satchel and compared the photo of the demolished house with the apartments. In the photo were two semi-detached two-storey white houses, with small front gardens behind an iron railing. This seemed the most likely location for Joyce's house (and a later look at an Ordnance Survey map from the early twentieth century confirmed it). There was something bleak about the tarmacked drive, unpainted aluminium railings and automatic gates of the apartment blocks – they looked unfinished, unhomely.

I passed a row of red-brick terraced houses where a middle-class family – a man and a woman with two very young children – was unloading a large car. As I passed, I noticed that the parents were carefully scanning the pavement to make sure that, in the few feet between the open car door and their open front door, nothing untoward or unexpected would occur.

The first lines of 'Araby', the third story in *Dubliners*, came to me as I rounded the corner: 'North Richmond Street, being blind, was a quiet street except at the hour when the Christian Brothers' School set the boys free.' The school is still there, along the west side of the street. Between 1894 and 1897 the Joyce family lived at number 13, a three-storey red-brick building that forms part of a terrace of houses running along the eastern side of the street. Joyce also describes a second house, an 'uninhabited house of two storeys . . . detached from its neighbours' that stood at the blind end of the street. That building, its lower windows barred against potential intruders, was now home to the offices of the Irish National Organisation of the Unemployed, and was named Araby House after Joyce's story. As I stood in the middle of the quiet cul de sac, I could see the steel exoskeleton of Croke Park looming over the rooftop of Araby House.

A pile of three black plastic refuse bags had been arranged in a pyramid outside the terraced house where the Joyces had lived. The house was divided into flats. A hall light glowed dully from behind the glass fanlight above the red front door. I stood on the opposite side of the street while a woman pushed a bicycle through the door and down the steps of Araby House. A cat, white with patches of grey and brown, ran across the street and made its way along the footpath. The woman paused to say hello to the cat, then cycled off.

From here, the Joyces moved a short distance north-east, across the River Tolka to Fairview. I turned left on the Ballybough road, in the direction they would have travelled on their journey from North Richmond Street. Crossing the Tolka at Ballybough Bridge, I thought of Father Conmee, the Jesuit priest who had been rector of Clongowes Wood when Joyce had attended, and who had been instrumental in getting Joyce his place at Belvedere. Joyce repaid the debt by portraying Conmee, his name unchanged, in both *A Portrait* and *Ulysses*. In the 'Wandering Rocks' episode of *Ulysses*, Conmee boards a tram that brings him towards Annesley Bridge, a little downstream from the bridge I was crossing. (The trams themselves are long gone.) The priest alights from the tram near Malahide Road, and as he walks his thoughts are drawn back to Clongowes: he remembers the feeling of the stubble of the school's fields on his feet. He's in two places at the same time.

With each move, the Joyces brought fewer items with them. As I walked, I tried to picture them walking across the bridge, framed pictures tucked under their arms, behind a horse and cart transporting their furniture. Their next home was on a quiet residential road called Windsor Avenue, whose two terraces of well-kept two-storey houses looked much as I imagined they would have done in 1897. A bike was locked to the railings in front of number 29, which was painted a grubby pinkish hue.

The Joyces lived at four addresses in Fairview in the space of four years, owing to John Joyce's distaste for paying rent. Stanislaus described the method his father used when a landlord wished to get rid of him: he would say to the landlord 'that it would be impossible for him with his rent in arrears to find a new house, and that it was indispensable that he should be able to show the receipts for the last few months' rent of the house he was living in'. The landlord would give him receipts for the unpaid rent and with these John Joyce 'would be able to inveigle some other landlord into letting him a house'. The years in Fairview corresponded to Joyce's time at University College Dublin, and in *A Portrait* Joyce describes Stephen's walk across the city from Windsor Avenue to the college on Earlsfort Terrace in the south city centre: 'The rain-laden trees of the avenue evoked in him, as always, memories of the girls and women in the plays of Gerhart Hauptmann . . . His morning walk across the city had begun.'

I needed coffee, and found a Centra opposite the junction of Windsor Avenue and Fairview Strand. The self-service coffee machine was out of order, but when a girl in a Centra uniform walked over to the machine I decided to loiter in the shop until it was fixed. I walked to the other end of the shop, near the second entrance to the premises. A security guard eyed me suspiciously. I thought that enough time had elapsed and went back to the coffee machine, which the girl was now dismantling, reservoir by reservoir. When she carried a large white plastic container away from the coffee counter, I cut my losses and left. I would find coffee somewhere else.

From Windsor Avenue the Joyces moved a short distance westward, to the corner of Convent Avenue and Richmond Road. I made my way past a couple of men in high-visibility vests who were guarding some wet concrete and arrived at the house I was looking for, a strange, hulking mass. The number on the door read '223' – indicating that this building was officially on Richmond Road, though the entrance was on Convent Avenue. I tried to scribble something about this into my notebook and I heard the rattle of plastic on pavement: I had dropped the lid of my blue Bic ballpoint. In the dull winter twilight, I couldn't find it.

Two families occupied the house in the Joyces' day; now, it was divided into four flats. Across the road was a recently built apartment block. It was cylindrical, five storeys tall and decorated with wooden panels on the ground, second and fourth floors – a series of closely aligned vertical slats fastened to an otherwise blank wall that stretched across to surround the small windows on the side of the building facing the road. Semi-circular balconies with glass barriers sprouted from the other sides of the building. I crossed the road and walked to the Esso service station, where I bought a coffee and a doughnut. I fished out my map of Dublin and rested it on a pile of peat briquettes before crossing the road and walking a very short distance down Richmond Avenue.

The Joyce house, number 13, is gone, and Richmond Avenue is now a spooky combination of industrial yards, tenement houses and newish gated apartment developments. As I stood there, taking in the strange juxtapositions in the barely illuminated gloom, I thought of the Norwegian playwright Henrik Ibsen, whose unremitting realism and hostility to social constraint influenced Joyce's fiction. Joyce had published an article entitled 'Ibsen's New Drama' in the *Fortnightly Review* while living on Richmond Avenue; Ibsen responded positively to the editor of the journal, who passed on the dramatist's response to Joyce. Not long after the publication of the article, the Joyces moved again. From the next address, 8 Royal Terrace, Joyce wrote a long letter in Norwegian to Ibsen to salute the writer on the occasion of his seventy-third birthday: he most admired Ibsen's 'wilful resolution to wrest the secret from life', his 'absolute indifference to public canons of art, friends and shibboleths' and his 'light of inward heroism'.

The darkness of Richmond Avenue was something

I wanted to escape. A large house at the end of the street, isolated in a builder's yard, seemed haunted by some inexpressible knowledge. Later, I discovered that this house had once been home to Thomas Clarke, signatory of the 1916 Proclamation, who was executed by the British forces in the aftermath of the Easter Rising.

Royal Terrace, since renamed Inverness Road, was no more than a hundred metres to the north as the crow flies, but the map indicated that getting there entailed a circuitous walk – south, east, north and west. I spotted an alleyway not shown on the map, leading behind some twentieth-century houses at the northern end of Richmond Avenue. I passed an old man slowly carrying his shopping and entered the alleyway, which was rubbish-strewn and dark. It took a sharp turn left. To my right was a gate at which stood a pair of startled dogs, who paused thoughtfully for a moment before barking at me. I was still carrying coffee and a doughnut, and wondered if they were hungry. I turned left out of the alleyway and on to Inverness Road – a walk of thirty seconds from the previous Joyce home.

The alley was a portal linking two dramatically different streets; for the first time, I had the impression that the Joyces' fortunes – or at least their surroundings – were improving. Inverness Road was handsome and well kept; number 8 was a large two-storey cement-clad house with a basement level and a hedge maze in the front garden. I thought of something Stanislaus Joyce had written about his brother: that he was able to grow and thrive in circumstances that seemed inimical to intellectual or artistic development, that it seemed 'little short of a miracle that anyone should have striven to cultivate poetry or cared to get in touch with the current of European thought while living in a household such as ours, typical as it was of the squalor of a drunken generation. Some inner purpose transfigured him.' The young Joyce seemed to maintain a kind of internal exile from the external squalor that was dragging the rest of his family down, one that preceded and predicted his eventual physical exile. Like Stanislaus, I wondered how Joyce was able to transmute a turbulent, deeply uncentred upbringing whose trajectory can be traced around the map of Dublin into a way of working and a mode of seeing that yielded some of the greatest works of literature in the English language.

I began to reconsider my plan. If I were to see all the Joyce addresses in one day, and in chronological order, I'd have to take a trip out of town, to the Martello tower in Sandycove, then return to the city centre. But it was already dark and cold, and I was exhausted, so I decided to visit the remaining addresses out of sequence.

After he left Dublin in 1904, Joyce returned just three times — once in 1909 and once in 1910 to what was then the family home near Broadstone; then in 1912, when he stayed at two addresses on the North Circular Road. On my way to Glengarriff Parade — where the Joyces moved after Royal Terrace — I would pass the North Circular Road addresses.

Joyce stayed in numbers 617 and 609 North Circular Road in 1910 and 1912 respectively, when they were known as 21 and 17 Richmond Place. I looked the two tall red-brick houses up and down and noticed that one of the houses between them, 613 in the current scheme, had its number written on the red-brick wall beside the front door in what looked like chalk but was probably Tipp-Ex. I thought about how many of the houses I sought had had their numbers changed, and how, if someone decided to change the number of 613 North Circular Road, they could do it with a paint scraper and a dab of correction fluid. I thought about how the names of so many streets had changed since Joyce's day, and about how if all the house numbers in Dublin were altered overnight, nothing would be too different except you'd have to have your post redirected and curious tourists wouldn't be able to find so easily the houses where James Joyce once lived.

When I reached Glengarriff Parade, I turned towards what I thought was James Joyce's house, and had the uncanny feeling of being followed . . .

After Glengarriff Parade, I walked in the direction of Phibsborough, where John Joyce took the previously unthinkable step of buying a house. While living at Glengarriff Parade, James's brother George had died of peritonitis, and Stanislaus Joyce believed the purchase of the next house, at 7 St Peter's Terrace (now 5 St Peter's Road), was fuelled by his father's regret over

George's death: 'My father, moved perhaps after Geor-gie's death by some transient twinges of conscience, commuted part of his small pension and bought the little two-storied house in Cabra and some indispensable furniture at auctions [. . .] My father moved into the new house with the usual programme of good intentions, but if he himself had any illusion that they would last beyond a fortnight, he was the only member of the family that had.'

James Joyce had graduated from university in October 1902, and immediately made plans to go to Paris, leaving Ireland on 1 December. John Joyce took out a mortgage on the St Peter's Terrace house to fund his son's visit home over the Christmas break. In April 1903 he sent James a telegram telling him to come home, that his mother was dying. In *Ulysses*, Joyce rendered the tele-gram from father to son in this way: 'Mother dying come home father'. Joyce spent the few months before May Joyce's death at home in St Peter's Terrace; she died in August 1903. After her death, the family fell apart. The St Peter's Terrace house was sold in 1905.

I walked through the crossroads at Phibsborough, taking a right down a flight of steps to the road that ran alongside what had once been a branch of the Royal Canal, leading to a basin at Broadstone, where goods were unloaded for businesses and wholesalers in the city centre. The canal branch was filled in during the 1920s, and is now a linear park that intersects the North Circu-lar Road. The houses along the west side of the old canal stand on a road called Royal Canal Bank. As a light mist descended to soften further the yellow sodium glare of the street lights, the serene silence unnerved me slightly.

I crossed the ghost canal and turned a corner to Fontenoy Street, a road lined by one-storey red-brick houses. John Joyce moved here from St Peter's Terrace with his six daughters – Margaret, Eileen, May, Eva, Florence and Mabel. James Joyce, who had by now made his home in Trieste with Nora, stayed with his father and sisters when he returned to Dublin in 1909 and 1910 – bringing his son, Giorgio, with him on the first occasion. Before leaving Dublin in September 1909, Joyce had signed a contract for his first book, *Dubliners*, with Maunsel & Co. He returned again in October, to help establish Dublin's first cinema, the Volta, which opened on Mary Street in December.

At 44 Fontenoy Street, a red-brick single-storey end-of-terrace house, I stopped. It must have been a fairly crowded household, particularly when James visited his father and sisters. I turned from the end of Fontenoy Street and made my way towards the building known as the Black Church – a former Protestant church built in 1830 that stands in the middle of the road near Parnell Square. Its real name, St Mary's Chapel of Ease, was supplanted by the popular local moniker – a reference to the dark stone of the jagged pinnacles and spires, or maybe to the legend that by walking anti-clockwise around the church three times at midnight you will summon the devil. Feeling not at all tempted to summon the devil, I trudged directly past the church and down the west side of Parnell Square.

I considered walking the length of O'Connell Street and crossing the river to Tara Street station in order to get a train to near my next destination before realizing I simply couldn't walk any further.

From O'Connell Street I got a bus to Ballsbridge. I walked down Lansdowne Road and turned left on to Shelbourne Road, where Joyce lived at number 60 in an upstairs apartment for much of 1904. Although he stayed at a couple of other places for a few nights during 1904, 60 Shelbourne Road was his main address. The house itself, in the middle of a brown-brick terrace, had large wooden-framed sash windows.

Chronologically, the next address at which Joyce stayed was at Dromard Terrace, in Sandymount. I checked the index of my pocket atlas of Dublin and noticed the address wasn't listed. Lacking a smartphone, I sent a text message to my girlfriend, who checked the address and responded with directions.

The journey to Sandymount village brought me across the railway line and past the Aviva Stadium, through streets of red-brick Victorian houses and past the village's triangular green. Against the dark horizon above the neat red-brick houses, I could see the flashing lights of the chimneys at the electricity-generating station at Pigeon House. In spite of the cold night, Sandymount's pubs and restaurants were doing a steady trade: laughter and chat emerged from them whenever a door was opened.

My girlfriend had given me directions from the coast road, so I walked north-east from the green towards the sea. Sandymount Strand, along which Stephen Dedalus and Leopold Bloom separately walk in *Ulysses*, was a dark expanse to my right as I strolled a short distance along the coast road before turning left on to Marine Drive, and left again into Dromard Terrace. The white plaster house at number 22 had been the home of the poet James H. Cousins and his wife, Gretta. On 15 June 1904 the McKernans, with whom Joyce had his room on Shelbourne Road, allowed him to leave and return when he could pay his rent, and he moved into a spare room at Dromard Terrace. This was Joyce's residence on 16 June 1904, the date which would assume totemic significance for Joyce and on which he would set *Ulysses*: it was the day that he and Nora arranged to meet to go walking in Ringsend – their first date. It was also the day Joyce, Richard Ellmann wrote, 'entered into relation with the world around him and left behind him the loneliness he had felt since his mother's death'.

From Sandymount, I took the DART to Sandycove, a village along the coast just beyond the port of Dún Laoghaire. I stepped from the train and climbed the ramp to the station entrance. Across from the station, a steep road called Islington Avenue slopes down to the seafront. At the foot of Islington Avenue, I turned right and walked along the curving coastline. By this time I had begun to hobble slightly. Ahead of me, the Martello tower, which was illuminated by floodlights, glowed like a beacon on the horizon – and Sandycove stretched out like an arm to embrace it. I shuffled along the path next to the road, the seafront promenade lit brightly to my left across an expanse of dark parkland. As I edged towards the headland on which the squat stone stronghold stood, the light from the lamp posts dropped away and I found myself walking in a gloom that for some moments gave me the feeling of being alone – but soon I encountered dark figures heading away from the tower.

The circular stone Martello tower at Sandycove was one of a number of robust defensive structures constructed during the British empire along its coastline, beginning in the years of the Napoleonic Wars. Around fifty were built along the coast of Ireland; fifteen of those guarded the short stretch of coast between Dublin and Bray. The towers were placed within sight of each other so signals could be passed along in case of attack. During the summer of 1904, Joyce's acquaintance Oliver St John Gogarty was renting the tower from the War Office for the sum of £8 per annum. (In *Ulysses*, Joyce has his alter ego, Stephen Dedalus, rent the tower, and the Gogarty character is the tenant.) At the time, Gogarty wrote to a friend that he had rented the building to 'house the Bard', as he called Joyce, who was working on his novel 'Stephen Hero', which was later to become *A Portrait*. Another resident, Samuel Chenevix

Trench, was a member of an Anglo-Irish family who had embraced the Irish cultural revival fervently. One visitor to the tower wrote of 'two men living in a tower . . . who were creating a sensation in the neighbourhood'. But Joyce stayed for just a few days in September 1904. Stanislaus believed that Gogarty wanted to turn Joyce out of the tower, fearing that he'd become a dependant, but that he was 'afraid that if Jim made a name some day, it would be remembered against him that though he pretended to be a bohemian friend of Jim's, he put him out. Besides, Gogarty does not wish to forfeit the chance of shining with a reflected light'. On the night of 14 September, Trench, woken by a nightmare in which a black panther was about to spring, grabbed his revolver and shot at the fireplace next to which Joyce was sleeping. Then Gogarty seized the revolver and shot at the pans above Joyce's bed. Joyce calmly dressed and walked from the tower to Dublin, a distance of some seven miles. When he came to write *Ulysses*, Joyce opened the book with a scene in the tower – the date shifted back in time to 16 June, the day he had first walked in Ringsend with Nora.

Within a few weeks of vacating the tower, Joyce had again departed from Dublin for Paris, this time in the company of Nora. The tower was a full stop, marking an abrupt conclusion to his time in Dublin.

The road veered past the Sandycove beach, and I followed it, walking up a narrow lane that led around the base of the tower. At the top of the lane, a car switched on its headlights and drove off in a hurry. I tried to decide whether I had interrupted furtive sexual shenanigans or whether the driver had simply panicked at the vision of a foot-dragging figure lurching up the hill towards the tower.

I was alone, standing between the soft glow of the floodlit tower and the subdued rumble of the tide. In the darkness beyond the tower, where the sky still held the promise of snow, Joyce would continue a grand adventure, in Paris and Pola and Trieste and Zurich – but the city that edged towards that darkness, the old city I had just travelled around, retracing the twisted path Joyce's family had taken from house to house, would never be forgotten by the writer, and would be reshaped and reborn, atomized and reconstituted in his work. The tower was the end, but also the beginning.

5. To the Lighthouse

The South Wall, also known as the South Bull, is a sea wall that stretches eastwards from the mouth of the River Liffey towards the centre of Dublin Bay, culminating at the red-painted Poolbeg Lighthouse. The wall is built from large granite blocks, and both sides of its base are protected by heaps of riprapped rock ballast. It measures 32 feet wide at its base and tapers to 28 feet on top. Its surface is flat and many leisure walkers can be found there in good weather; swimmers and fishermen also use the wall.

One bright, sunny day, I set out to walk across the industrial badlands of Poolbeg Peninsula and onward to the wall's end. The peninsula is as man-made as the wall, its land reclaimed from the Liffey estuary, and is, in fact, counter-intuitively, a more recent creation. The wall dates back to 1715, when the Dublin City Assembly, seeking to prevent the silting up of the River Liffey, voted to begin the construction of an embankment along the South Bull sandbank. The original South Wall consisted of a row of wooden piles driven into the boulder clay of Dublin Bay, anchored by baskets of clay and woven wattles. The piles ran from near the current site of the electricity-generating station and were linked to Ringsend by the stone Ballast Office Wall, completed in 1756. It soon became clear that the piles were prone to rotting and tidal stress, so in 1761 work began on a granite wall to replace them. The Liffey's silt problem persisted until another wall was completed on the north side of the river, in 1825.

While narrow strips of land were reclaimed around the South Wall in the nineteenth century to house a military fort, a hospital and a short-lived hotel, most of what's now known as the Poolbeg Peninsula is a product of the twentieth century. The ribbon of lumpy parkland that stretches across its southern shore is composed in large part of the rubbish dumped there when it served as a municipal landfill. Council houses, too, were built on some of this reclaimed land, and in their early years there were problems with rising gas generated by the rotting rubbish below. A local resident, Joe McCarthy, told me that the women who lived in those houses 'never needed a clothes dryer'; instead 'they'd spread their clothes on the floor because the floor was hot because of the combustion going on, the slow combustion in the municipal dump below them. They were hot for the first ten years they were living there.'

Poolbeg is the place where the necessary functions of the city – container port, electricity generation, sewage treatment – go to hide. The dump is no longer active, but a waste incinerator is planned. Although very much a part of Dublin, and not far from the city centre, Poolbeg feels separate, raw, unfinished, provisional. Yet in this it is merely a slightly distorted mirror image of the city as a whole. It was reclaimed from the sea, but so were more central areas of contemporary Dublin. Up until the eighteenth century, the area east of present-day Tara Street was, for the most part, sloblands: a muddy meeting of the Liffey, the Dodder and Dublin Bay. Sir John Rogerson's Quay was constructed as a private development in the early eighteenth century; subsequently, the marshy land south of the quay reaching eastwards to the Dodder was divided up into plots and in 1723 each was sold to the highest bidder. This area became known as the South Lotts. City Quay was completed in 1820, allowing the reclamation of the area north-east of Trinity College. Much of the land to the north of the Liffey was, similarly, reclaimed during the early eighteenth century. The street names communicate something of this lost geography: Townsend Street to the south of the river, Newfoundland Street (now erased from the map, having been built upon) to the north. Before the south-side reclamations, Ringsend – the largely residential district that adjoins the Poolbeg Peninsula to the east – was an isolated spit of land that could be most easily reached from the city by boat.

On a map or satellite photo, the peninsula's outline is suggestive of a pistol aimed eastwards into the sea. From west to east, it is around three kilometres in length. At its widest western point, where it meets the mainland, it's around 750 metres from north to south; that tapers down to a little over a hundred metres at its eastern tip, and then again to the narrowness of the South Wall.

Starting from Sandymount, to the south-west of the peninsula, I walked along Seán Moore Road, then turned right at a large roundabout. This is, roughly, where the peninsula begins. Following Pigeon House Road south-eastwards, I passed the north-eastern boundary of the enormous site formerly occupied by the Irish Glass Bottle Company plant – now fenced off and overgrown.

Behind the Glass Bottle site's black perimeter hoardings was a row of fully grown trees, but the barriers were so tall – perhaps 15 feet – that all but the treetops were hidden from view. The site was fortified, secure, but through the gate I could see an undulating landscape of gravel and rubble. Beside the gate was a large, bright notice in blue, yellow and red on a white background; it advised building contractors of the safety procedures on the site. But there was no one to be seen – nothing had been built, nothing was being built.

In October 2006, the site was bought for €412 million by a consortium led by a major property developer, Bernard McNamara. The Dublin Docklands Development Authority, a public body charged with leading the regeneration of the once-moribund docklands, joined McNamara's consortium as an investor. At a meeting held on 24 October 2006, the day before the closing date for receipt of tenders for the site, the DDDA's executive pointed out to its board that the proposed bid for the Glass Bottle site would be made at the 'top of the market' and that the Irish commercial market was 'overheated'.

The minutes of the meeting record no further discussion of these questions, and no detailed analysis of the risks seems to have been carried out. At the time, the board was led by Lar Bradshaw, who had in 2004 been made a director of Anglo Irish Bank; Anglo chairman Seán FitzPatrick also sat on the DDDA's board. Perhaps not coincidentally, Anglo supplied more than half of the loan finance for the consortium's acquisition. The bank had also committed to putting a further €898 million into the development of residential, office, commercial and retail property on the site.

The DDDA executive's call of the top of the market turned out to be more or less correct. Before long, the market turned, and McNamara (like most of the other big developers) was unable to service his debts. The Glass Bottle site had been purchased for a figure that would never be recouped. In January 2011, not yet five years after it had been purchased for €412 million, the site was valued at €45 million.

Some time after my walk across the Poolbeg Peninsula and along the South Wall, I visited the DDDA's headquarters, situated along the median, or campshire, between the road and the river on Custom House Quay. I had an appointment with Loretta Lambkin, the authority's chief executive. She told me the authority had done a huge amount of good; she also talked about how things had gone wrong, particularly with regard to the Glass Bottle site. A giant map of Dublin's Docklands took up an entire wall of the reception area. In front of it was a black wooden plinth which held a dashboard-like panel of buttons. Each button corresponded to a certain area of the map – but the buttons weren't working.

A few days after I visited the DDDA, I met Joe McCarthy, a resident of Sandymount who had been actively opposing the proposal to build a rubbish incinerator on the peninsula. At one point in our discussion, Joe seemed to question the ownership of the Glass Bottle site, referring to a previous transaction in which the site had been sold by the Earl of Pembroke. There is a school of thought that the land had never properly belonged to the earl in the first place. It was a legally arcane subject, but one thing was clear to me. When we discussed the Glass Bottle site, we were talking about land that was fewer than forty years old, reclaimed from mud and sand at the mouth of the Liffey. Ireland was young, but the Poolbeg Peninsula was younger, and its fortunes reflected those of the independent nation. I thought about the land at Poolbeg that had – let's assume – belonged to the Earl of Pembroke. In the twelfth century the 2nd Earl, nicknamed Strongbow, helped the deposed King of Leinster regain his crown and then married his daughter. He was granted Irish land: this was legitimate under Norman law, but not under the Brehon law that the Irish clans observed. Who owned the area around Ringsend before Strongbow arrived from across the sea? Was it possible that the land was taken back from the people who took it in the first place? But then I reconsidered: the majority of the land along the peninsula was reclaimed, mostly after Ireland had gained its independence. Forty years ago, the Irish Glass Bottle Factory site was a city dump. Who, then, owned the peninsula if not the refuse-producing nation? In a sense, it was as close as you'll ever get to authentic independent Irish land: built on rubbish, overpriced, unattractive yet unaccountably coveted, and sometimes even loved.

On the opposite side of the road from the Glass Bottle site, beyond a sloping grass bank and a security fence, cargo containers sat stacked in ziggurats coloured blue, red and grey like giant steel Lego blocks. The road was strewn with broken glass of uncertain provenance and each side of the desolate avenue was lined with T-shaped, reinforced-concrete barriers that resembled anti-terrorist defences but were actually there to discourage Travellers from parking their caravans. (This is something they did in the past, both on this road and further along the peninsula.) This stretch of Pigeon House Road seemed unhomely, a corridor of flux through which everything passes without stopping.

Just past the freight yard, the main road took a ninety-degree left turn while another branched off into a dead end among sites occupied by large storage tanks and yards, cement-processing plants and additional stacks of cargo containers. I followed the main road left along the perimeter of the main container yard, taking a sharp right on to a long, straight stretch that brought me past more storage tanks and, on my right, a small electricity-generating station, which was followed by the site intended for the waste incinerator. (By January 2014, Dublin City Council had spent €95 million on the project, €50 million of which had been paid to buy the site at Poolbeg, and it was still not clear if the incinerator would ever be built.)

Beyond that was Dublin's main sewage-treatment plant – a place I would visit on a separate expedition. A scattering of older structures dotted the road, including, to the right, just before the sewage plant, an old red-brick building on a wedge-shaped site which was, in 1903, converted to a hospital facility for smallpox sufferers. Further on, directly opposite the entrance to the sewage plant, were the stone and brick remnants of a military fort built after the 1798 Rebellion, while a hotel nearby, built in 1793, was requisitioned for military use. The fort remained operational for almost a hundred years. A landmark along the South Wall is the eighteenth-century Ballast Office storehouse, completed in 1761; its first caretaker was one John Pidgeon, and the building became known as Pidgeon's House or, eventually, the Pigeon House.

I continued past the large granite hotel building, which was now overshadowed by the red-brick hulk of the original electricity-generating station; then I took a sharp right at the main gate leading to the Electricity Supply Board's site, alongside which three cannons were angled towards oncoming traffic in sinister tribute to the area's military heritage. When I glanced to my left, I could see the two huge red-and-white-striped concrete chimneys of the now-disused power station stretching skywards.

It's difficult to overstate how visible the Poolbeg chimneys are from almost everywhere in the city, or how dramatically they punctuate a cityscape that is otherwise lacking in dramatic landmarks. People returning to Dublin by plane often say that seeing the chimneys heightens their sense of arrival. The chimneys are tall, and isolated, and their visibility is enhanced by the red and white stripes that are intended to make them conspicuous to passing aircraft. And, while the chimneys are sited close to the easternmost point of the urban core, they're also oddly central when you take into account the geography of Dublin Bay: from Howth Head or Dalkey, you can look back westwards at the chimneys, the sight lines across the bay uninterrupted by anything except occasional mist or fog.

Though visible from all sides, the chimneys are also curiously inaccessible: if you want to go there, you really have to make an effort. And then, when you stand on the road below them – beside the scrubby ground with a sign that says 'Irishtown Nature Park', not far from the concrete tanks of the sewage plant – you find yourself overwhelmed by the scale of them.

The chimneys stand as remnants of a key stage in the development of power generation on the Poolbeg

Peninsula. In 1892, Dublin Corporation opened an electricity works at Fleet Street, in the area now known as Temple Bar in central Dublin. Prior to this, there were a number of smaller private attempts to provide power to the city. In a large industrial-looking building on Fleet Street, huge steam-driven wheels and belts created just enough electricity to supply the immediate area. Although there were some problems – notably when rubber insulation around cables decayed and had to be replaced – in general, demand was high and the operation was a success. Meanwhile, the townships of Rathmines and Pembroke developed their own supply, using direct current rather than alternating current, ruling out the possibility of standardization. The ESB's official history speculates that this was in order for the two townships to maintain independence from the city.

Demand for electricity grew, and a larger site was needed for a new power station. By September 1903, it had opened and the plant at Fleet Street shut down. The distance from the load centre had forced Dublin Corporation to use a three-phase, four-wire system which subsequently became the global standard for the supply of electricity.

The red-brick generating station, which still stands, resembles a large warehouse with a squat brick chimney at its southern end. In its early years, the station was cutting edge: on a winter day, a shift staff of eight men operated the plant, which generated 20,000 horsepower, burning 200 tons of coal every 24 hours. Because of the station's location, coal could be easily delivered by ship, and water for cooling and condensing was plentiful.

In 1929, the ESB took control of the power station. In the 1950s, a new plant was built along Pigeon House Road, but first it was necessary to reclaim acres of land on either side. In the ESB's archive, I looked at an aerial photo taken in 1951 that shows two large square patches of land facing each other across the road, enclosed from the sea by a wall and filled with earth. A later photo, taken in the 1960s, shows the new plant – known as the Ringsend plant – up and running: a sleek and modern building whose bright turbine hall and futuristic-looking control room seemed a world away from the belts and wheels of the Fleet Street station. Commissioned between 1955 and 1957, the Ringsend generating station was further expanded in 1965 and 1966. Demand for electricity was growing, and an official pamphlet about the Ringsend station mentioned a future generating station called 'Pigeon House B'. This was to become the Poolbeg station.

In 1966 the head of Civil Works at the ESB, Maurice O'Sullivan, read a paper to the Institution of Civil Engineers of Ireland about reinforced-concrete chimneys. The paper, although a model of clarity, was very much the work of an engineer: it concentrated on the optimum height of chimneys (not less than two and a half times the height of the boiler house, to avoid flue gases being drawn to turbulence around the building) and how to protect concrete chimneys from acid corrosion (a full-height lining of acid-resistant brick with a four-inch space between the concrete outer layer and the inner brick lining). It's clear, though, that at the time the paper was delivered, power stations were becoming larger and chimneys were, consequently, growing taller – at least two and a half times the height of the new, bigger boiler houses.

The first two units of the Poolbeg plant (and the first chimney) were completed in December 1971; the third unit (and second chimney) in November 1978. All ran on oil and gas. In an interview with a local newspaper, Brian Segar, a steeplejack who worked on the maintenance of the Poolbeg chimneys, described how they were constructed using a system called a slip form: a circular mould was made, into which concrete was poured; once that concrete was dry, the mould was moved upwards and filled with more concrete. In this way, a seamless series of concentric concrete rings were stacked, forming a chimney. The chimneys stand like sentinels at the entrance to Dublin and are far more visually striking than their creators can have envisaged.

The Golden Gate Bridge and the Empire State Building have their own epic tales of construction. I was curious about the story of the Poolbeg chimneys. That's how I found myself sitting opposite Maeve O'Sullivan as she talked to me about the life and work of her father, Maurice. Although she was at pains to point out that many other people within the ESB worked on the chimneys, Maeve told me that she thought her father had been 'the main designer' of the second chimney, and had been involved in the design of the first as well. She also told me that she had a friend whose brother had also worked on the design. 'And my friend's kids were calling them "Uncle Jimmy's chimneys", you know? And we'd be calling them "Daddy's chimneys".' The day after I talked to Maeve, I sat in a bar with a friend of mine who also knew someone who had helped with the construction of the chimneys.

When the Poolbeg plant was decommissioned in 2010, there was a public outcry – people wanted to keep the chimneys. But no one's sure exactly what the future holds for them. Unlike the 1903 Pigeon House power plant, the Poolbeg plant is not listed as a protected structure: if the ESB wanted to knock the chimneys down, it could. When I asked local councillor and former Lord Mayor Dermot Lacey about their status, he told me that the ESB had agreed not to interfere with the structures without informing Dublin City Council of their intentions, at which point, he said, 'we will immediately seek to have them protected'. A number of smaller and more efficient turbines continue to run on the site next to the decommissioned plant.

When I talked to Maeve O'Sullivan, she quoted to me something that her dad used to say about construction: that 'people relate to tall structures'. Certainly, in Dublin – a low-rise city where few buildings come anywhere close to the height of the chimneys – the twin poles of Poolbeg provide a seemingly ever-present navigational guide on the eastern horizon. It seems unthinkable that they could be demolished.

Around the corner from the ESB entrance, stretching along the south bank of the peninsula, is a broad, sandy strand beloved of kite surfers. At low tide, it sometimes appears as if you could walk from the strand directly across to the beach at Sandymount. North of the strand, beyond the perimeter fence, the two giant chimneys of the generating station seemed much closer to me than before, and I began to get some idea of the scale of the buildings: the enormous generating halls at the base of the structure were dwarfed by the towers.

Along the road adjoining the strand there is a disused bus stop, a vestige of a recently cancelled service that transported workers to the peninsula and ran just a couple of times a day, in the mornings and evenings. Beyond the strand, I passed a gigantic tank in which some of Ireland's oil reserves are stored. When I turned away from that tank, eastwards towards the Irish Sea, I began to walk along the granite blocks of the South Wall.

At the western end of the wall, just south of the pathway, is a small patch of land, on which I could see the remains of a few ruined buildings. A little further along the wall is a blocky stone building which seems now to be used as a boathouse. From this building a pipeline once discharged sewage from the townships of Rathmines and Pembroke into the sea at high tide. The pipeline opened in 1881 and the machinery was operated by the Costello family, who lived in a house on the now-ruined adjacent site.

The Half Moon Swimming Club is based in a white-washed former gun battery about halfway along the South Wall. The club takes its name from the shape of the building, which curves slightly, a design intended to accommodate a gun turret. A little while after my walk along the wall, I met up with a senior member of the club, Ben Kealy, who had been going down the wall to swim since he was a child in the 1940s. He's now the chairman of the club, and still swims in the sea along the South Wall during the summer months.

I asked him what had changed along the Poolbeg Peninsula since he began coming here. 'I started school in the Star of the Sea in Sandymount. That would have been 1941. And there was a dump there then. The dust-bin carts used to go down there, dump the stuff. A really awful place.' He told me how some of the rubbish would occasionally break free of the dumping area and be washed into a strip of fast-flowing water between the wall and Sandymount: 'It used to miss where we are and it used to head around the lighthouse and on out with the current.'

Ben Kealy also told me about the Poolbeg Lighthouse at the end of the South Wall, which is now automated but used to be manned by a number of lighthouse keepers, who were kept entertained during the summer months by people wandering along the wall. 'There'd be always gangs of people walking down in the evenings in the summer. And the lighthouse keepers used to sit out on the seat. One of them was known as the Major, and he had a monkey. Vicious little bastard. He was quite famous for that. There were four lighthouse keepers. And they worked three weeks on and one week off. They stayed down there for three weeks. If you go down to the lighthouse you'll see the remains of an old hoist crane, just on your left-hand side. That's where they used to lift up the supplies for the lighthouse keepers.'

Unprompted by me, he mentioned how much he hated the 'awful bloody chimneys' of the ESB power station. I had been under the impression that most people were fond of the chimneys.

'There's talk of taking them down now,' I said.

'Oh, I wish they would,' he said. 'They're awful.'

As I walked along the wall, and further and further from the city, the buildings around O'Connell Bridge began to disappear into the haze behind me, leaving only the upper floors of a few taller office blocks visible. The closer I got to Poolbeg Lighthouse, the easier it became to imagine that the city wasn't actually there. Perhaps this is why people are drawn to walking the wall: the feeling of the sublime that strikes the solitary walker at a physical remove from the urban, and surrounded by water.

Part of writing about a place is imagining what it might be like if it weren't there at all.

I reached the lighthouse and followed its curved wall

around to the eastern side, where, below me, a lone fisherman stood on the rocks, casting his line to the sea. I looked at the choppy water and thought about climate change and rising sea levels, and I wondered how long this wall, and the Poolbeg Peninsula, would last. The peninsula had been built upon potato peelings and broken umbrellas and unfinished meals and old, unwanted sofas; it had been used to channel sewage into the sea. Coal and gas and oil had been burned here to generate electricity, and, if Dublin City Council eventually had its way, rubbish would be burned for the same purpose.

The South Wall had been an audacious attempt to divert nature for the good of the city, and a successful one at that. I turned back in the direction of the city centre and saw fumes billowing from the electricity-generating station, while a huge container ship passed along the channel towards Dublin Port. It seemed unlikely, in that moment, that something could be done to save Poolbeg's waste lands from their apparent fate, but I awaited the next grand plan.

6. Down the Drain: On the Trail of the City's Sewage

A long, straight road, lined with well-kept bungalows and new two-storey dwellings, leads down to the sea at Loughshinny, a small village on the coast of north County Dublin. The road bends left at a stone wall that bears a simple plaque reading, cryptically, 'Plane Crash Tayleur'; the plaque commemorates a plane that crashed into the bay in 1913 and a ship, the *Tayleur*, that ran aground on rocks in 1854. Beyond the stone wall and across a sandy strand, you can see a stretch of blue sea leading to Lambay Island. The road brings you to a car park that adjoins the strand. Beyond that is the harbour, defined by a stone pier stretching from the north and a jutting headland to the south, where you can usually find a couple of small fishing trawlers at anchor.

When I reached Loughshinny, I turned away from the strand and the curving cliffs and clambered over the harbour wall. On the other side of it, I found a rocky, rubble-strewn shore that was largely hidden from view. About a hundred metres along stood a low concrete bunker, from which a concrete pipe led into the sea. It was late afternoon, and the tide was fairly high: the pipe was visible in the shallows before disappearing into deeper water. I climbed to the top of the bunker and sat down.

The concrete was warm in the afternoon sun. Through a manhole cover, I could hear the rushing of liquid below me. I inhaled the acrid stench of raw human waste.

Before my trip to Loughshinny, I had read a report published by the Environmental Protection Agency on Ireland's wastewater treatment plants and outlets. The report included a map marked with hundreds of little green and black triangles, squares and circles, each representing a point where effluent is pumped into rivers, lakes and seas in the full range of possible states. What flowed from this bunker on the beach into the Irish Sea was untreated sewage.

When we think of sewage, we tend to think of human excrement. Drainage professionals use the term 'wastewater', and this is not a euphemism; it reflects the fact that most of what enters the sewer system *is* water: from showers, sinks, washing machines, dishwashers, toilets, industrial processes, and rain, which enters the network via outdoor drains. But most of what makes wastewater offensive and dangerous, if it is not efficiently drained and treated, arises from the presence of human shit.

The largely invisible underground network of pipes that carries wastewater from our homes generally goes unnoticed until something happens to make us aware of its presence. When I was a teenager, a blocked pipe caused the backyard of my family's house in south Dublin to fill with sewage; with my mother, I waded through the dull, brown water in wellies, attempting to solve the problem, before we finally called in professionals, who unblocked the drain with high-pressure hoses. But most of the time, for most people who live in modern cities in wealthy countries, the sewage system runs smoothly, invisibly. Along every street in practically every city around the world, however, there are rivers of foul liquid flowing just beneath the surface.

In *The Big Necessity*, her 2008 book about the management of human waste around the world, Rose George pointed out that almost 50 per cent of sewage in Ireland was treated only to primary levels – screened for lumps – and called Ireland a 'rich country with an infrastructure more suited to a poor one'.

My trip to see the Loughshinny pipe confirmed this judgement, as did a glance at the EPA map that showed hundreds of similar outfall pipes around the country.

Before Dublin had a sewer system, the city's streets often served as open drains; cesspools full of sewage festered behind houses and bred disease. In 1773 and 1774, legislation was passed and a board formed 'for paving, cleaning, lighting, draining and improving the streets'. New sewers were paid for by rates levied on residents. Householders on certain streets would occasionally refuse to cooperate and, as a result, those drains weren't laid, remained incomplete or were filled in.

In Braithwaite Street in the Liberties in 1798, the Reverend James Whitelaw found severe overcrowding (for example, four families sharing one apartment) and swarming vermin. He recorded that human waste was flung from the windows of the buildings into the backyard, building up in tall heaps that reached to the first floor. When it rained heavily, the heaps of shit would ooze on to the streets, as 'there is not one covered sewer in that populous portion of the Liberty south of the street called the Coombe'. And the problem was not restricted to the Liberties. Dublin's most significant thoroughfare, Sackville Street (later O'Connell Street), had cesspools as late as 1816.

By 1849, some 35 miles of sewers had been constructed in the city. In 1851, Parke Neville was appointed borough engineer and local surveyor; in 1857, he became Dublin's first city engineer. Between 1851 and 1879, Neville built 65 miles of new sewers, and improved around 30 miles of older drains. These sewers were mostly built of brick and were known as 'three by twos' – around three feet in height and two wide. They drained into the River Liffey from fifty-four outfalls between Islandbridge and Ringsend, polluting it badly. Some of the drainage infrastructure built in the nineteenth century remains in use: Robert Buckle, the Dublin City Council area engineer with whom I walked the Poddle tunnel, told me about what he believes to be the oldest intact sewer, dating back to 1852 and still in use in Cornmarket.

The Dublin Main Drainage Scheme, completed in 1906, saw the construction of large-diameter sewers under the Liffey quays which intercepted the majority of the sewage that had previously flowed into the river. The north sewer crossed beneath the river near Eden Quay, joining the south sewer in its progress towards the newly constructed processing plant at Ringsend. In 1958, the North Dublin Drainage Scheme was completed: a large sewer now ran across the north of the city from Blanchardstown to Howth, where untreated sewage was pumped into the sea. Some coastal areas of Clontarf are downhill from the main pipe, so pumping stations were used to drive the wastewater up to the main line. Although the main purpose of the North Dublin Drainage Scheme was to alleviate overloading in the existing north Dublin sewers, it also provided capacity for the expansion of the northern suburbs.

In the 1960s, a new network of sewers was built around Dún Laoghaire, while the earlier Victorian-era drains were improved. Subsequently, this system was overtaken by population growth in the area, with the consequence that overflows of unprocessed sewage were regularly released on to the coastline. In the 1970s, a large sewer was built along the south bank of the River Dodder in south Dublin, running from Tallaght to Ringsend. This high-capacity drain took wastewater from the suburbs located between the mountains and the southern city – Templeogue, Rathfarnham, Churchtown, Dundrum – while also enabling the growth of residential and industrial areas in the western suburbs. The Grand Canal Tunnel, which runs five kilometres from Dolphin's Barn to Grand Canal Street, has the same internal diameter as a London Underground tunnel. Following recent extensions, it now brings sewage to Ringsend sewage plant from as far away as Ratoath in County Meath – a distance of 27 kilometres.

In 1998, an undersea tunnel was constructed to run from the pumping station at Dún Laoghaire across Dublin Bay to Ringsend, in an effort to eliminate sewage discharge to the coast. Two years later, an extensive network of sewers was built across the north fringe of Dublin, skirting the M50 motorway and reaching from Finglas, through Santry and Coolock, as far as a pumping station in Sutton, from which an underwater pipeline was built across the bay to Ringsend, consolidating the treatment of sewage from the north and south city in a single plant. As late as 1999, sewage sludge from the Ringsend plant was dumped from barges into the sea in the vicinity of Baily Lighthouse, just off Howth Head.

When I started thinking about what happens after we flush our toilets, I pictured a central control room where sewage could be tracked as it moved through the city, and wondered if such a thing existed. It turns out that it does, more or less.

Alan Vickers works in the Drainage Services Division of Dublin City Council. When I met him in a conference room at the council's offices, he powered up his Panasonic Toughbook to show me what was going on in the sewers. At certain key points in the system, there are what Vickers calls 'flow monitors' – sensors that track the flow, depth, pressure and volume of sewage moving through the pipe. The flow monitor consists of a metal band around the inner circumference of the sewer pipe, with sensors positioned at twelve o'clock, three o'clock, six o'clock and nine o'clock. The monitors send signals back to the Drainage and Services Division's computer system, alerting the council to take action if the volumes are too high; they also enable the council to tally volumes of wastewater coming from other councils in order to charge them for the use of the plant in Ringsend. If the flow monitor indicates unusually high volumes of sewage, or slow-moving sewage, drainage workers will be sent out to check on it.

Vickers picked up his mobile phone and dialled a local number. The call was picked up on its first ring and answered with a squall of electronic noise similar to what you hear when you dial a fax number. This noise was coming from a modem connected to a sensor in the sewers: each sensor has its own phone number. New technology meant that more recent sensors could use wireless SIM-card-based systems. Some sewers had landlines; others had mobiles.

A few days later, we went to see the sewer Vickers had dialled. We found it under a small manhole in a housing estate in Chapelizod. We had been driven there by Christy Maguire of the Drainage Division, who lifted the manhole using a long, crowbar-like iron tool which he called a 'key'. I looked into the opened sewer. The pipe was about double the diameter of the nine-inch pipe that could be seen joining the main sewer at an angle, carrying wastewater from the rows of houses south of where we stood. A moderate amount of brown liquid flowed at a gentle pace through the main sewer below. There was little, if any, discernible smell. Just inside the manhole, attached to the ladder rungs leading down to the pipe, and looking like a car battery with cables sprouting from it, was the part of the flow monitor that communicated with the green box at the end of the street.

In a sports field in the grounds of University College Dublin, we looked at a much larger sewer, 1.5 metres in diameter. Vickers and Maguire levered the shamrock-shaped manhole cover, this time using two keys they'd brought for the purpose. Below us, the contents of the Dodder Valley sewer drained at high speed in the direction of Ringsend. There was a strong smell of excrement, with strange notes of bleach or washing powder. Vickers later sent me velocity data from both drains: the flow of wastewater through the UCD sewer reached as much as 2.2 metres per second, or nearly 8 kilometres an hour, while the Chapelizod sewer was much slower – about 0.4 metres per second, or 1.44 kilometres an hour. The greater volume of sewage and the incline of the Dodder Valley pipe account for its greater speed.

Vickers told me that during periods of heavy rainfall the pressure in the sewer at UCD had been known to become so great that the manhole cover – which took two people to lift – had been blown off and sewage and other detritus spread to a distance of ten metres around the opening. I had spent a largely uneventful period studying in UCD, and it struck me that this was by some distance the most exciting thing that had ever happened on the campus.

A few days later, I visited the wastewater-treatment plant at Ringsend. Michael Kenny, Dublin City Council's senior engineer at the plant, led me through a pair of tall metal doors beside which was a sign, black text on yellow background, that read: 'Stop odours please keep doors closed'. Inside the low-slung building, the noise was relentless, and we had to raise our voices to make ourselves heard. A series of grey metal machines stood along one wall. Industrial metal panels served as a floor, below which channels of raw sewage rushed. This was where the treatment of Dublin's wastewater began.

'There's seven channels, and it all comes through here, and then these are the screens,' Michael said, 'what we call bar screens, loads of bars, and there's a six-millimetre gap between the bars. So when the water flows through, the solids – or the rags, as we call it – get caught on the screens, and rakes come up and just rake off the screens.' He gestured towards a machine he'd opened up. Long metal combs with serrated teeth drew sodden grey shreds of material from the foul water below.

'When I say rags, this is what I'm talking about. It's like baby wipes and –'

'Stuff that doesn't get broken up?'

'Yeah, sanitary towels, condoms, all that kind of stuff.'

There are seven of these machines, one for each

channel of sewage hidden below the flooring. In normal conditions, only three machines are kept running at a given time, but at times of heavy rain – when, Michael told me, the flow of wastewater can increase fourfold – they might have all seven going. If the flow was heavier than the plant could handle, some of the sewage could be redirected to storm tanks on the other side of Pigeon House Road, where it could be stored until levels returned to normal, at which point it would be pumped back into the system.

We walked out of the building. Below us, you could hear water rushing, and to the left was a series of covered tanks – the grit tanks, where inorganic material is removed from the process. 'The first thing we do is take the screenings out, or the rags,' Michael told me. 'And the second thing is to take the grit. The grit is basically what gets washed off the roads. It's like sand or small little stones. If they are passed forward into the process, they increase the abrasion in the pumps and all the mechanical equipment.' Fats, oil and grease are also removed from the wastewater at this stage.

Whatever sinks to the base of the tank is spat out by two large plastic tubes into a long, grey skip. Without getting any closer than was necessary, I had a look at the black-brown heaps of grit that had built up in the skip. There were stones there, as I'd expected, but the grit heaps were also dotted with a startling number of bright yellow specks that stood out against the dull background. It took me a second to realize what I was looking at.

'You do get some organic stuff like sweetcorn,' Michael said.

I was now feeling slightly unwell. That sweetcorn had passed through the digestive systems of Dubliners.

Once the sewage has passed through the grit tanks, it's pumped into one of twelve primary treatment tanks, which separate solids from liquid. The primary treatment tanks used at Ringsend are a type known as lamella tanks. Michael Kenny told me that inside each one there are plates mounted at an angle to accelerate the settlement of the solids, and that there are scrapers at the bottom of the tanks that move the solids to one side. When the original plant opened in 1906, the scraping of sludge from the primary settlement tanks was done manually – an undoubtedly disgusting job for which I hope, but doubt, someone got well paid.

Although there was a persistent sickly smell at the Ringsend plant, I hadn't noticed any wildly offensive odours. This was because of the odour-control efforts that had been made on the site. Sprouting from each lamella tank was a huge green metal tube that drew air from the tank and pumped it through a purification system. Michael told me that the air inside the tank was changed four times an hour. This system was installed in 2008, in response to long-standing complaints about odours by people who lived nearby; since then, the number of complaints has dropped significantly.

When the sewage has settled in the lamella tanks, the

liquids are channelled away and the sludge is pumped into a holding tank, from where it will be drawn for further treatment. As the liquids still have an amount of suspended solids floating in them, they're sent for secondary treatment in huge tanks called sequencing batch reactors.

We stood in the open air at the base of a steep metal staircase that led up one side of what looked like a concrete multi-storey car park. The dull grey sky stretched south towards the Dublin Mountains, just visible on the horizon. The sound of bubbling water was audible from the tanks above, which were exposed to the elements.

'You're not afraid of heights?' Michael asked.

'Not really, no.'

Perhaps I should have been more honest. I don't like heights. When I climb to an altitude above a couple of storeys, my inner ear starts to spin. But I had gone to considerable effort to secure this guided tour, and so I decided to follow Michael up the steep metal staircase. It brought us to a narrow platform above a network of twenty-four tanks, each seven metres deep, and stacked on two levels. I was wearing a pair of safety glasses, a hard hat and a high-visibility jacket; although the possibility wasn't discussed, I assumed the latter would be handy for locating me if I fell into a tank of sewage. I looked across the site of the plant, back towards the city. To my left, I could see Sandymount Strand curving southwards. Behind me, the open tanks of wastewater bubbled through their treatment cycles. Beyond them, the imposing chimneys of the old Poolbeg power station reminded me that heights were relative. As Michael spoke, I took notes, juggling a pen, a notebook and a digital camera. Having my hands full in this way made me worry about dropping my pen into the mire below.

To my left, the surface of a tank full of murky water simmered as if being boiled, while to the right another tank was perfectly still, its glassy surface reflecting the sky. Michael explained what I was seeing: 'There are twenty-four tanks – twelve on this level, twelve on the level below.' Each level is broken into three sets of four tanks, working in sequence. 'So in the four tanks the sequence is: fill, aerate, settle, decant. In each group of four, you'll have one filling, you'll have one aerating, you'll have one settling, and you'll have one decanting.'

We walked across a metal bridge that brought us directly above the tanks, the dark liquid just beneath our feet. Huge pipes roared next to one, bubbling tank. This is aeration, which is achieved by pumping air through wide-diameter pipes into the base of the tank. During settlement, the remaining suspended organic material gathers together and falls to the tank's floor. Decanting consists of lowering the walls of the tank in order to tip the cleaner water from the surface while leaving sludge at the base – like tipping the boiling water off pasta when it is cooked. Once the water is gone, the equivalent of a plug is pulled and the sludge drips away, joining the sludge from primary treatment in a holding tank.

Michael told me about what he called 'bugs' – micro-organisms that digest the organic waste in the water – and how they're naturally present in the sewage; you just have to create the right environment for them to flourish.

I was having trouble processing this information. I had expected a complex chemical operation.

'So the micro-organisms are already in the sewage?' I asked.

'Yeah, they are.'

'So it's about creating the right environment for them.'

'Yeah, exactly.'

This is what aeration does – the micro-organisms need oxygen to thrive. Michael explained that there are two kinds of micro-organism that are relevant to the process. The first kind – anaerobic digesters or the eaters – ingest solids; the second kind – the sinkers – gather around the eaters and cause them to plunge to the bottom of the tank.

Having crossed the metal bridge, we descended on the east side of the tanks, the Poolbeg power station side. To our right, a green pipe led out from the tanks to a building where the water is treated with UV light, which kills bacteria and pathogens, before being pumped out into the mouth of the Liffey through an outfall pipe that runs under the power station.

Michael and I walked from the stack of bubbling tanks to the other side of the site. The next stage of the process takes place in a building full of tall chrome canisters surrounded by piping. The canisters look like enormous milk pails, thirty feet tall. Michael explained that they act as huge pressure cookers that treat the sludge, in a process called thermal hydrolysis. This leaves the sludge molecules primed for the anaerobic digesters which, as he put it, 'eat the solids' and produce methane gas.

The digesters consist of a set of four wide, grey silos that stand next to the thermal-hydrolysis building. The sludge is pumped from there, brought to a temperature of around 38 degrees Celsius – body temperature – and then propelled into the digesters, which break it down further, into solids and biogas. The biogas then passes into a storage balloon, which resembles a huge golf ball, and used to power an electricity generator, which feeds power back into the grid. Michael tells me this process generates enough power to cater for 'between 50 and 60 per cent' of the plant's energy usage. The steam produced by electricity generation is fed back into the thermal-hydrolysis process.

I walked across the gravel and touched the gas balloon. It felt like the unevenly patterned surface of a basketball. When you pushed against it, there was a slight give – as if the basketball hadn't been fully inflated.

The solids are pumped through a surprisingly narrow silver pipe from the digesters into a nearby building, in which they are heated in rotating ovens to a temperature of 450 degrees Celsius – several people I talked to referred to this process as 'pasteurization'. Michael told me that they were the same kind of ovens that were used by Guinness to roast hops. The solids are then sent through a cyclone system that recycles the air from the process, and brought by a covered conveyor belt up an incline to a modified grain hopper that hangs over a loading bay outside the building. This spits the dried solids into an open, skip-like haulage trailer parked below.

Later, this dark material, with a consistency now somewhere between a powder and a pellet, will be driven away to be used as fertilizer on farms in Carlow, Kilkenny, Tipperary and Wicklow.

At the drainage desk in Dublin City Council's headquarters, you can consult a list called the Sludge Register, which gives details of all the people who've bought the dried fertilizer produced from sewage sludge in Ringsend. In its dried state, the product is frequently referred to as biofert. When the product hasn't been dried and exists in a wet form, it's referred to as biocake. Both biofert and biocake are also referred to as biosolids. As I read through the Sludge Register, I noted the names and locations of people who had bought biofert – mainly farmers in largely rural counties, but also the odd one in the rural west of County Dublin, and a couple of GAA clubs in Wicklow.

According to the Environmental Protection Agency's 2012 report on urban wastewater, 106,788 tonnes of sewage sludge was produced nationally in 2009; 62 per cent of this was reused in agriculture. But the use of biosolids is controversial. A number of leading food organizations and companies – including Bord Bia, Glanbia, Dairygold Co-op and the Irish Grain and Feed

Association – enforce bans on the use of biosolids. Glanbia told me that its policy of opposing the use of sewage-derived fertilizer is 'consistent with the Irish Grain Assurance standard'. Tom Kelly, of the Irish Grain Assurance Scheme, an umbrella group for grain production in Ireland, emailed me about biosolids, saying that 'there are too many "unknowns" with this product, therefore there is a potential food safety risk. This could have the potential to cause very serious damage to our industry. Most end users have a ban on this product and therefore most merchants also have it banned. They will monitor council applications to apply the product and therefore the grower may find he/she has no market for their grain.' In 2008, the Food Safety Authority of Ireland (FSAI) published a report on use of municipal sewage sludge in agriculture that included this sentence: 'given the uncertainty of treatment processes for reducing virus levels in sewage sludge and the extended transit distances reported for viruses, the most significant public health threat would appear to come from the use of sewage sludge (either treated or untreated) in close proximity to watercourses'. When I discussed the 2008 report with Dr Karl McDonald of the FSAI, he said that there had been 'a commercial decision by certain companies' not to allow the use of biosolids, but that he believed 'the controls for use are more than sufficient'. The traffic of sewage through Poolbeg forms part of a cycle: the sludge produced at the treatment plant is reused as fertilizer to help grow food which residents of greater Dublin eat and excrete. Their sewage in turn is flushed through the city's underground network of sewers to the Poolbeg plant, and so the cycle continues.

During the nineteenth century, the reuse of sewage in agriculture was often seen as a viable way of saving perfectly good manure from being flushed away into rivers and seas. Victor Hugo bemoaned this waste: 'Science, after having long groped about, now knows that the most fecundating and the most efficacious of fertilizers is human manure,' he wrote in a section focused on the Parisian sewer system in his novel of 1862, *Les Misérables*. 'Certain success would attend the experiment of employing the city to manure the plain. If our gold is manure, our manure, on the other hand, is gold. What is done with this golden manure? It is swept into the abyss.' Around the same time, agricultural fields west of Paris began to be irrigated with sewage piped from the city. However, Hugo might have overstated the nutrient load of human manure: a Swiss report published in 1999 shows that sewage contains under 3 per cent of the nitrogen, around 10 per cent of the phosphorus, and less than 0.2 per cent of the potassium usually contained in animal manure.

In 1868, Dublin Corporation asked Joseph Bazalgette, the chief engineer of London's sewer network, to comment on a proposal for the reuse of Dublin's sewage for agricultural purposes. This plan suggested that iron pipes, suspended above the ground, should run along the banks of the Grand Canal, distributing sewage which farmers could collect for use on their land. Although medical advice was against residences being within two and a half miles of land treated with sewage, Bazalgette noted approvingly that 'I have for several years past resided within one and a half miles of the meadows irrigated with the sewage of Croydon. Villa residences of superior quality have been, and are rapidly being, built around the very margin of this sewage farm.' He wrote that it has been 'practically demonstrated' that sewage can be 'profitably applied to agriculture'.

In 1983, Dublin Corporation acquired a ship named after Bazalgette and used it for dumping sludge into the sea.

Since 2005, the Greater Dublin Drainage project, a coalition led by Fingal County Council which includes the other Dublin councils and those of Meath and Kildare, has been planning the development of a new sewage-treatment plant in north Dublin and a significant orbital drainage system stretching from the city across the northern part of the county. The project was deemed necessary to facilitate the expansion of the greater Dublin region, to comply with environmental legislation and to take pressure off the treatment plant at Ringsend. The Ringsend plant handles the vast majority of the Dublin region's sewage and is currently being expanded; but, owing to a lack of available space at the site, it will be unable to expand significantly in the future. According to maps provided by Greater Dublin Drainage, the proposed orbital sewer will run eastwards from Blanchardstown, parallel to the M50 motorway, stretching as far east as the area of largely rural land between Portmarnock and Clongriffin. Two northern branches will diverge at the Finglas M50 interchange and at Kinsealy. Those branches will run to the east and west of Swords before meeting up to the north-west of the town, from where the sewer will head north-east, passing north of Lusk and Rush before arriving near Loughshinny.

In October 2011, nine locations were listed as potential sites for the sewage plant. By May 2012, that list had been whittled down to three. Two were near the rural town of Lusk in north County Dublin; one was on the edge of the city at Clonshaugh, not far from the airport. There were two potential outfall locations, both draining into the Irish Sea: Portmarnock and Loughshinny. Only one location would be chosen.

A few weeks after my first visit to Loughshinny, I sat around a table in a community centre – a converted schoolhouse – with several members of the Loughshinny Community Association. On the table, Marian Bentley, a member of the association, had spread a number of maps of the area. 'They've changed the position of the outfall pipe,' she said. 'The original one was supposed to be beside Drumanagh,' a headland just south of Loughshinny. 'They just keep moving stuff around here, there. There's no explanation, or there's no logic to it.'

One of the maps showed two green lines – the path of the proposed pipeline – leading towards an area of land north of the harbour. Here the lines joined a wide, rectangular box whose borders were green and which was scored with diagonal lines, also green. The rectangular box stretched a couple of centimetres into the sea, while a small amount of land along the coast was also covered. This was the proposed area for the outfall sewer.

Barry Rice looked at the map to see where his farm was located – 'It'd be just kind of roughly ... it'd be roughly along here, now. It's obviously only a small bit of the coastline' – and pointed to the land covered by the green box.

Soon after meeting the Loughshinny Community Association, I went to Lusk, a village in rural north Dublin, to meet Lorcan O'Toole, a member of a group called Lusk Waste Watch, who was going to show me the two proposed locations for the sewage plant near Lusk. He met me at the station and talked as he drove, calling the proposed sewage plant 'a Celtic Tiger vanity project'.

On an earlier trip through the area, I had seen greenhouses, carefully ploughed fields and signs that read 'No sewage plant here'. Locals felt that Lusk had been unfairly targeted, that Greater Dublin Drainage was already committed to a process that it was unwilling to adjust or abandon. In general, local people I talked to felt that smaller-scale local sewage plants were the answer. Everyone else I spoke to – mostly workers in the wastewater industry and academic researchers – said the exact opposite, that 'big is best': more manageable, more economical, more energy-efficient, less prone to breakdown. While residents in rural fringe areas are more familiar with either small sewage plants or none at all – many have septic tanks, unconnected to a drainage network, that are cleared of solid waste at intervals by tanker trucks, which generally dispose of those solids at sewage-treatment plants – there's a strong argument for replacing those solutions with a larger plant that takes urban, suburban and rural sewage and processes it to a level that's environmentally acceptable.

When talking to the campaigners at Loughshinny and Lusk, I was told repeatedly that the statistics provided by Greater Dublin Drainage were wrong. I was handed alternative statistics drawn up by the protestors which diverged widely from the official figures. One graph predicted that, due to a variety of factors, the required sewage-processing capacity for the Dublin area would, by 2031, be almost exactly equal to that in 2012. A 2012 report by Greater Dublin Drainage, by contrast, provided three growth scenarios which predicted an annual growth rate of between 1 and 1.4 per cent between 2011 and 2040.

Lorcan O'Toole and I drove to the first site at Newtowncorduff, a field not far from the M1 motorway. We then turned left, passing his house, which is about five hundred metres away from the proposed site. We crossed the bridge to the other side of the motorway and, having passed along a narrow country road for some distance, we looked through a gate towards some trees. This was the second site. I found it difficult to imagine what it would be like if a large sewage plant were located in either of these places; it was clear that locals refused to imagine it.

The opposition to the creation of new sewage infrastructure in north County Dublin betrays a deeply held anxiety about what the future might look like, about what might or might not happen when a plant is finally built. This is why locals wanted to know how big the plant would be and what would occur if things went wrong. It's why facts were queried, rubbished or distorted and speculation took over. In this context, official prediction became just another guess about what could happen twenty or thirty years from now. Everything became science fiction.

It was clear, too, that the residents of Loughshinny and Lusk thought of their communities as rural. They were supported in this view by Fingal County Council's development plans, which designated the area as green-belt. Yet the populations of the area had also noticeably expanded as a result of residential development, giving some towns a distinctly suburban atmosphere.

When I met Peter O'Reilly, the chief engineer of the Greater Dublin Drainage project, he acknowledged that the project was partly about the expansion of the city. He compared it to the enlargement of Dublin's sewage system in the 1970s, which accommodated the growth of the new western suburbs. In the absence of that new infrastructure, he said, the city 'couldn't have developed. In Blanchardstown, where you've got about 200,000 people and a lot of industry, you couldn't have developed it, because you wouldn't have had the infrastructure. And, if you like, this is where we're going now, taking the next leap in providing for the future.

'We're providing for the long-term development of the metropolitan region,' he told me. 'If someone comes along and they want to locate an industry, we're competing with Singapore, we're competing with Israel, we're competing with Arizona.'

It seems that there's no simple answer to what we should do with our sewage. I began to think about it as having a lot in common with nuclear waste: treated, buried, stored but, most of all, feared. There were possible health risks. No one wanted it, but it had to be dealt with somehow. And what happened if something went wrong?

Dublin had directed its wastewater through Ringsend for over a century; in that hundred or so years the city had sprawled and the Ringsend plant had expanded to handle the increase in sewage volume. Sewage plants have always operated below capacity most of the time – it's the only way to ensure they can accommodate extra volumes during flooding, or to allow back-up machinery to kick in if something breaks down. To have a single large plant operating at, or even close to, capacity in an expanding city is risky.

To get some sort of idea of what a new north Dublin sewage plant might look like, and smell like, I went and sat on a wall in a stretch of parkland next to the

Shanganagh sewage plant, which is sandwiched along the coast of south County Dublin between the DART railway line and Killiney Bay. The plant, which is smaller than the one proposed for Lusk, was built in 1996 to cater for its local area. It has recently been upgraded so that, now, no processes are carried out in the open air. A housing estate adjoins the plant, and a row of houses ends about a hundred metres from it; the gap between the last house and the plant's perimeter wall is filled with garden allotments. Behind a low-lying building, I could see a large white sphere – the gas balloon. There was no smell, as far as I could tell. It struck me that when Bono flushed his toilet, this was where his waste would end up.

A man wearing a broad-brimmed hat walked by with a playful black Labrador. As the dog chased a tennis ball, I asked the man about the plant. He said it used to smell, but since it's been upgraded he hasn't smelled anything. He also told me that you could sometimes see a blue flame, like you'd see on a gas cooker, burning in one of the chimneys. I later found out that this happened in the early days of the upgraded plant, before the gas was fully utilized for generating electricity on site – they would burn off excess methane.

In June 2013, Greater Dublin Drainage announced that it had decided to locate the new sewage-treatment plant at Clonshaugh, with the outfall pipe entering the sea near Portmarnock. The sites chosen for the plant and outfall both lie on the border between Fingal and

Dublin city. The Dublin city side of the border consists of a mixture of housing estates, shopping centres and industrial estates, while the Fingal side is largely agricultural: fields, trees, hedgerows. Tommy Broughan, a local Fine Gael TD, called the decision 'a cynical power play by the politicians in Fingal' to place on the fringes of Dublin city a plant that would primarily serve the people of Fingal. The Fine Gael Minister for Health, James Reilly, whose constituency includes the parts of rural north Fingal that would have been directly affected by any other decision, cautiously welcomed the choice of site. Local councillors suggested that Greater Dublin Drainage should fund community projects to compensate local residents for the burden of taking on such an undesirable piece of infrastructure. The day after the decision was made, I emailed Lorcan O'Toole to find out how he felt. He told me that 'the relief in Lusk is fantastic' and that, on hearing the result, he had felt 'like a child who had just opened his Christmas presents'. He was keen to express sympathy for residents in Clonshaugh.

Meanwhile, raw sewage continues to trickle into the sea from a rubble-strewn beach behind the harbour wall in Loughshinny.

7. The Bus Game

I used to make the journey from my parents' house to university – an awkward trans-suburban trip that could not be comfortably completed without changing buses once – using a Travel 90 ten-journey ticket. The small print on the back of the Travel 90 points out that the 'final journey must start within 90 minutes of boarding the first bus'. Because I had only ever used the ticket for my commute – two buses in the morning and two in the evening – I hadn't really considered the broader possibilities of the Travel 90 until one Sunday afternoon a few years ago, when I needed to pick up a couple of books I had left in my office at University College Dublin. I was travelling from my girlfriend's house, and because it was Sunday, and the traffic was quiet, I was able to reach the campus quickly, in just over half an hour. Once I had collected the books, I returned to the bus stop, caught a bus to the city centre and then another south to my parents' house. I didn't have to wait long at any of the stops – there wasn't much traffic – and I got on the last bus within ninety minutes of boarding the first; so I had taken four buses for around the cost of a single trip.

Sometimes it feels as though the city and its infrastructure are designed to drag you down: sluggish buses, trams and trains; heavy and aggressive traffic on the roads; dawdling pedestrians who get in your way when you're in a rush. But once in a while, things go right: the pavement opens up in front of you, all the lights seem to turn green, or your train pulls in on time. That Sunday journey across the city to my office got me wondering if it was possible to turn bus travel into a game, a means of exploring the city in a different way. To be fun, a game needs rules, limitations; and here was where the Travel 90 came in. How many buses, I wondered, could you travel on within the ticket's ninety-minute window, and how far could you go?

I took a small piece of paper – small enough when folded to fit into my wallet – and wrote out a list of rules. Firstly, I would choose a starting point: a bus stop some-where in the city. I'd get the next bus that came along, validate the Travel 90 ticket and start a stopwatch. I'd get off the bus ten minutes after I had boarded, flip a coin, then catch the next bus in the same direction or in the opposite direction, depending on whether the coin came up heads or tails. After ninety minutes, the journey would be over: if I were on a bus, I would get off at the next stop.

I liked the idea of travelling across a city in a way that wasn't dictated by necessity, and I liked the idea of using public transport to bring me to an unpredictable destin-ation. These might have been eccentric enthusiasms, but they were not wholly original. In the 1950s, the Situa-tionist International, a Paris-based avant-garde group,

engaged in what they called the *dérive* – a playful drift
across the city which members would make by foot, or
sometimes by taxi, often having no idea where they'd
end up. The aim was to jolt participants out of habit and
routine and into a new awareness of the city. The Situationists thought of the *dérive*, which could last several days,
as a kind of utopian escape from the city's increasingly
divided functions of work, travel and leisure – alienating
divisions that often entailed a distance that had to be
overcome through commuting. It was both an explor-
ation of the more marginal locations of the city and a
pub crawl. One account of a *dérive*, by Guy Debord,
begins in this way: 'On Tuesday, 6 March 1956, at
10 a.m., G.-E. Debord and Gil J. Wolman meet in the
rue des Jardins-Saint-Paul and head north in order to
explore the possibilities of traversing Paris at that latitude.
Despite their intentions they quickly find themselves
drifting towards the east and traverse the upper section
of the 11th arrondissement, an area whose poor commercial standardization is a good example of repulsive
petit-bourgeois landscape.' Debord and Wolman continue through the 11th and 20th arrondissements, finding
themselves 'facing the impressive rotunda by Claude-
Nicolas Ledoux, a virtual ruin left in an incredible state
of abandonment, whose charm is singularly enhanced
by the curve of the elevated subway line that passes by
at close distance', before continuing north beyond the
boundaries of Paris into its suburbs, stopping at some
bars along the way.

Initially, the Situationists hoped their attention to the psychological effect of the urban environment on individuals – which they referred to as 'psychogeography' – would influence urban planning. A Dutch member of the group, Constant Nieuwenhuys, created intricate models of cities – typically glass and metal structures suspended on pillars above ground – and at one point members of the group attempted to attract financiers to fund their designs, proposing the construction of a Situationist city called Utopolis on an uninhabited island off the southern coast of Italy. But the models remained unbuilt.

In the late 1960s, the writer Georges Perec, who was a member of Oulipo, a group dedicated to investigating the use of constraints in the composition of literary texts, conceived of a project called 'Lieux' ('Places'). He chose twelve locations in Paris that were important to him, and drew up an elaborate schedule for the completion of the project. Each month, he would visit one of his places – the street he grew up on, for example, or the roundabout at the place d'Italie next to which a shopping centre was being built – and produce a text consisting of notes of what he observed there. In the same month, he would write a separate text based on a memory he had of one of his chosen places. He would do this for twelve years, producing a total of 288 texts. However, after a few years, Perec began to rebel against the scale of the task he had set himself – or, perhaps, found it too boring – and he never finished it.

From long experience, I was aware how soul-gnawingly

frustrating Dublin's public transport system could be. Perhaps approaching public transport in the playful spirit of the Situationists and with some of the discipline of Perec would unveil a hitherto undiscovered potential in the system. I envisaged the possibility that, having changed buses a number of times over a ninety-minute period, I might end up in a part of the city unknown to me. At the same time, I was aware that, in the Situationists and Perec, I was drawing from two approaches to the city that had ended in boredom and failure.

For my first trip, I wanted to begin in the centre of things, so I chose O'Connell Street, the city's busiest thoroughfare.

The question of which side of O'Connell Street to stand on was resolved by a flip of a coin as I crossed the west side of O'Connell Bridge. The coin came up heads so I remained on the west side, stopping at the first bus stop I came to, outside Eason's. There I would wait for the next bus that came along heading north.

I waited ten minutes, and a number 123 arrived – a yellow-and-blue-liveried double-decker. The 123 runs from Walkinstown, a suburb south-west of the city centre, to Marino, north-east of the centre. I had never been on this route before. I validated my ticket, started my stopwatch and climbed the stairs to the upper deck.

It was around midday, and the traffic was light as the bus took a right from O'Connell Street on to Cathal

Brugha Street, then, in short order, a left and a right. The route felt knotted and slow and, as the bus idled at the junction of Parnell Street and Gardiner Street, waiting for the light to turn, I wondered if I'd make it out of the city centre before I had to ring the bell and get off. I looked at my watch – five minutes to go. As I sat there and my anxiety grew, I wondered why I was so concerned with the bus's progress: after all, I had nowhere in particular to go and ninety minutes to get there. Nevertheless, until the bus finally accelerated away from the inner city, I was edgy. Instead of allowing me to break away from the more mundane aspects of public transport, it seemed the rules of this game intensified the vexation of bus travel.

By the time the bus had travelled up the narrow red-brick thoroughfare of Philipsburgh Avenue, in Marino, my ten minutes had run out. I got off at the next stop, flipped a coin: it came up tails. I crossed the road, but could see no stop on the opposite side. I walked north, following the route of the bus I had alighted from, but there was no sign of any stops, which led me to think that the 123 took a different route on its inbound leg. A smartphone would have clarified matters at this point, but I didn't have one. I reckoned that, if I could trace the outbound route, I'd eventually come across an inbound bus stop on the opposite side of the road. I continued to walk north up Philipsburgh Avenue, past a row of shops and some old two-storey houses.

At the intersection with Griffith Avenue, I crossed to the only bus stop I could see, next to the entrance to the Marino Institute of Education. I fished my cheap mobile phone from my satchel and texted the number of the stop to Dublin Bus's Bustxt service, which sent me details of the next three buses due to arrive there – all were 123s heading for Marino. Looking eastwards along Griffith Avenue, I saw, a hundred or so metres away on the other side of the road, a stop at which a handful of people had gathered. Although the group was small, it illustrated in microcosm Dubliners' attitude to queuing for the bus: they don't do it. Instead, oddly amorphous gatherings of anything from three people to, at busier city-centre bus stops, several dozen spread themselves across the pavement near the stop. When the bus approaches, there is some speculative manoeuvring as the more desperate or clued-in travellers attempt to judge where it will stop. Those who judge correctly are rewarded with being among the first few on the bus, while the rest wait their turn in the scrum on the pavement, shuffling slowly towards the doors. Needless to say, an orderly queue would speed up the whole process and be fairer, but it would be contrary to the ways of Dublin, and I can't help but feel it would detract from the festive anarchy you invariably encounter at the city's bus stops.

I crossed the road and waited at what had to be the inbound stop. When the bus arrived, a nervy young woman attempted to push a buggy through the door, but it got stuck, and she apologized to the driver. He tried to put her at ease. 'Don't panic,' he assured her. 'When I panic, you'll know it's time to panic.'

The bus turned left along a narrow suburban road that led to a large circular park surrounded by curved terraces of pebble-dashed two-storey houses. The area was calm and pleasant – as the people who designed it had surely envisaged. In 1922, plans for new housing developments in the Marino area were published as part of the 'Dublin of the Future' document – authored by a number of town planners from the University of Liverpool and commonly known as the Abercrombie Plan, after one of them. The Abercrombie Plan sought to reduce the populations of the slum areas, razing the buildings and relocating the residents to new 'garden city' suburbs. The authors employed town-planning lessons learned from company-built schemes in England such as Port Sunlight and Bournville, which created picturesque developments of houses set in a semi-rural environment of parks and tree-lined avenues; the idea was to improve the moral and physical health of the working classes. Influenced by the nineteenth-century town planner Ebenezer Howard's ideas, the Abercrombie Plan proposed that Dublin's new garden suburbs should employ a radial design, a network of circles and closes centred on a circular park. The Marino streets through which the 123 took me were a fairly pristine example of this project, largely intact the guts of a century on, although many of their front gardens had been paved to accommodate cars – the mass ownership of which hadn't been anticipated in the 1920s.

The bus made slow progress through the narrow roads and tight curves of the estate, and as it rejoined the lower reaches of Philipsburgh Avenue, I became aware of my ten minutes slipping away yet again. Mentally I urged the bus onwards. Again, I was responding like a commuter in a rush.

Ten minutes had elapsed by the time the bus crossed the Royal Canal, so I rang the bell. The stop was opposite a grocery store that listed its latest bargains in handwritten notices penned in permanent marker on large sheets of paper taped to its front windows. Across the road there was an untidy terrace of red-brick two-storey Georgian houses, most of which appeared to have been divided into flats. Nearby, a few steps from where I stood, Summerhill Parade met the busier North Circular Road. I flipped a coin: tails.

I had stumbled upon a weakness in my system. If I were to cross the road, as I was meant to whenever the coin turned up tails, I would have to get a 123 towards Marino again – there were no other buses on this route. As much as I liked Marino, I feared getting stuck there as a result of this unforeseen collision of short, isolated routes and a game that I'd designed under the evidently faulty assumption that most bus stops would serve multiple routes. If I kept flipping tails, I could end up ricocheting between Marino and town all day. I felt like a ball bearing trapped in the corner of a pinball table, bouncing back and forth but unable to descend towards the flippers.

Maybe I could break the rules? I recalled playing pinball years ago, in the dank UCD bar. When you wanted to dislodge the ball, you could jiggle the table. If you did this too violently, the game would punish you for it and freeze up, but the odd nudge was acceptable.

I decided to shake things up. Instead of crossing to the opposite stop and taking the next 123 in the direction of Marino, I would turn left on Portland Row – a leg of the orbital route that becomes the North Circular Road – and walk to the junction with the North Strand road, the closest alternative radial route. Perhaps the bus routes available there would give me more joy.

The junction between Portland Row and North Strand Road is known as the Five Lamps, after an elaborate wrought-iron lamp post with five lanterns that was erected in 1880. There, I turned left towards the nearest visible bus stop. Two tracksuited men were standing at the stop. One of them was holding two golf clubs: a putter and a nine-iron. He swung these, one in each hand, as if they were the blades of a windmill. I gave him more than enough room to continue this exercise, while keeping a wary eye on him. As a result of my distraction, I let a number 15 sweep by without stopping. I hailed the next bus, a 27B, and the driver shook his head as he regarded the man, who had not ceased furiously windmilling his golf clubs.

The bus brought me north-eastward, past Fairview

Park and then along the Malahide Road. After ten minutes, I got off at the Artane roundabout – at which point, flipping tails for the third time in a row, I crossed the road to wait for the next bus towards town. I wondered about the probability of flipping tails three consecutive times, wondered whether it was something to do with my coin-throwing style, then promptly forgot about the question when a packed number 27 arrived. The 27 runs from Clarehall in the north-eastern suburbs to Jobstown in Tallaght, a journey of around 25 kilometres. I hailed the bus, and sat upstairs at the front. The bus was packed, and by the time it reached Fairview, ten minutes later, schoolchildren were sitting on the stairs. I flipped a coin. Tails again.

I crossed the footbridge linking Fairview Park to the other side of the broad main road. The bus stop was bathed in the scent of fish and chips from a nearby takeaway. A bus arrived: a 14. I jumped on, as my stopwatch ticked towards ninety minutes.

The bus brought me again along the Malahide Road. My heart sank at the prospect of another visit to the Artane roundabout. But the 14 turned left on to Collins Avenue, and across to Whitehall. I got off the bus, and flipped a coin. Tails.

I crossed to the stop on the opposite side of the road. I had just seen a bus go by. I had five minutes to go before my ninety minutes had elapsed. I stood there and watched the traffic pass, and, when my time was up, I reset my stopwatch and walked away.

*

A hundred years ago, the number 16 tram ran between Drumcondra and Terenure, via Aungier Street in the city centre. Today, the number 16 bus, which I often use, follows an identical route between these two locations (but also extends north to the airport and south to Ballinteer). The replication of the old tram line is not a coincidence: tram routes in Dublin were replaced by bus routes.

Dublin's first tram line, from College Green to Rathgar, opened in February 1872. That line and the many that followed were built by a number of private companies, and the earliest trams were drawn by horses. The first electric tram journey took place in 1896, and on 13 January 1901 the last horse-tram in Dublin ran to Sandymount. The Dublin United Tramways Company (DUTC), owned by the businessman William Martin Murphy, acquired many of the smaller tram companies, and by 1905 it had assumed control over the majority of the network.

On 26 August 1913, tram workers deserted their vehicles in opposition to Murphy's anti-union policies. The DUTC had made contingency plans for a strike: inspectors and office staff, many of them former tram drivers, took over the operation of the trams. Pickets were placed on trams and services were curtailed in the evenings because of attacks, yet within a few days of the beginning of the strike a relatively normal daytime service was in operation. On Saturday, 30 August, workers stoned a tram in Ringsend, initiating a riot that spread along Pearse Street and across the river to the area around Liberty

Hall, the headquarters of the Irish Transport and General Workers' Union (ITGWU). During the rioting, two union members were beaten to death by police. When a mass rally scheduled for the following day was banned by the viceroy, the head of the ITGWU, Jim Larkin, went ahead with it regardless, addressing a crowd from the balcony of the Imperial Hotel on Sackville Street – an establishment owned by Murphy. Larkin was arrested and police baton-charged the crowds, injuring hundreds. More riots ensued. In September, a consortium of Dublin's employers, led by Murphy as president of the Dublin Chamber of Commerce, organized the 'locking out' of all their employees who were members of the ITGWU, and asked all other employees to sign forms dissociating themselves from members of the union. Supported by money and food supplied by British trade unions, the strikers held out for months. But the workers didn't have the resources to prolong the strike further, and British unions were unwilling to support a general strike. By January 1914, Larkin had admitted the failure of the strike and advised workers to return to work, a move which involved signing the forms dissociating themselves from union activity.

The DUTC continued to acquire tramways until the late 1920s, by which time Dublin's transport system was changing yet again. The first public bus services began operating in 1906, and expanded notably in the period after the First World War. The private companies that operated the bus routes were referred to as pirates, because they were unregulated and therefore free to undercut tram fares. As there wasn't yet a municipal bus system, the pirates could operate as they saw fit, making use of the public road with the same rights as any other motor vehicle. Fierce competition between the pirates on popular routes led to hair-raising races along the main roads into the city. Service was erratic – routes came and went – and subject to the whims of the drivers and the operators. These buses were generally single-decker flatbed vehicles whose capacity varied and whose condition was often lamentable. A photo of a pirate bus in the early 1930s shows a single-decker that wasn't much bigger than a small van. It has a protruding engine at the front, with small circular headlights on either side of the engine grille and mudguards that arch back from the front wheels before resolving themselves into running boards which formed a step for passengers. The bus's destination – Walsh Road in Drumcondra – is posted above the windscreen. The driver's compartment forms part of the roofed and glazed main cabin, in which passengers were seated. In the photo, a group of men wearing hats and coats stand on the road next to the empty bus – it's not clear whether they're waiting to board or observing the aftermath of an accident. Other buses were less sleek, and appeared to be flatbed trucks with passenger cabins built on top.

According to P. J. Flanagan and C. B. Mac an tSaoir's book *Dublin's Buses*, if a regular customer failed to turn up at a stop, it wasn't unusual for the driver to call around to that customer's house to see if they still wished to get the bus. Breakdowns were frequent, and when these vehicles had reached the end of their working life, they were dumped in a 'bus graveyard' between Old Bawn and Bohernabreena, just south of Tallaght.

The pirates were taking advantage of the fact that the legislation covering the DUTC didn't allow the provision of bus services except in highly defined circumstances. (As many railway companies owned hotels, this exception existed to allow them to run bus services to their hotel from a nearby railway station.) New legislation in 1925 extended DUTC's remit to bus services, and a timetable from November 1927 lists twenty-five tram services and fifteen bus routes operated by the company. The Road Transport Acts of 1932 and 1933 restricted operators to certain specified routes, and allowed the DUTC to acquire those of private operators working within its area – defined as within 15 miles of the General Post Office. In this way, the DUTC was able to secure what was effectively a monopoly on bus and tram services in Dublin. The expansion of bus services in the city was mirrored by the decline of the tramways, and although trams enjoyed a brief revival during the Second World War as a result of fuel rationing, the service ceased in 1949. On 1 January 1945, the DUTC – the 'T' now stood for 'transport', reflecting the company's diversification into buses and the decline of the trams – merged with Great Southern Railways to form Córas Iompair

Éireann, a company that was soon nationalized to become the Irish state's national transport provider.

The decline of the tram coincided with the expansion of ownership of the private motorcar, and Dublin's road traffic became a problem – and, apparently, a threat to the mental health of bus drivers and conductors. In 1958, CIÉ's medical officers suggested as a topic of investigation 'neuroses in bus crews, a greater problem in Dublin than in rural districts'. But this does not seem to have been taken seriously and, in 1962, the company moved to introduce one-man buses that would not require a fare-collecting conductor. This led to a strike in April and May of 1963. The then chairman of CIÉ, Todd Andrews, who was attempting to modernize the company but regretted the 'failure to bring the bus workers along with us', suggested that the Tavistock Institute make a study of the 'underlying causes of the poor morale of the busmen'. In 1967 the Institute's study appeared under the title 'The Morale of the Dublin Busmen'.

The report attributed the malaise suffered by busmen to the stresses and alienation experienced when travelling day in, day out in the relatively heavy traffic of an expanding city. The researchers observed bus runs and interviewed drivers and conductors. Some conductors criticized drivers' erratic driving, while the researchers observed conductors being overwhelmed and missing fares when a bus became overloaded or when there was a high rate of turnover of passengers travelling a short distance. Drivers would speed between stops or leave early from the terminus in order to make up time. 'Morale is low,' the report concluded. My four brief trips on the 123 bus made me wonder whether the mysterious malaise that officials had sought to diagnose had not simply been the inevitable result of grimly repetitive bus journeys taken over the course of a day.

The shift from tram to bus signalled a move towards investment in road transport, especially the private car. A little while after the tram system was dismantled, a vision for new towns in the west of the city was elaborated: distant from the city and dependent on car ownership. An assumption underpinned transportation provision for these suburbs: that most people would be able to afford cars. 'Throughout the free world, urban populations are "voting with their wheels" on this basic matter, and there is every sign that as prosperity grows Dubliners will do likewise,' Myles Wright wrote in 1967, in the first part of his report on the Dublin region.

My father got our family's first car in 1980. Before that, we had depended on buses or the kindness of neighbours or strangers who had cars – and we were still dependent on public transport when my dad was at work. I remember running with my mother along the Greenhills Road near Kilnamanagh to catch a navy and cream CIÉ bus in the direction of Tallaght village. (It must have been before 1987, because Dublin Bus was formed in that year, splitting from CIÉ.) It could be one of memory's fabrications, but I believe that we boarded the bus from a platform at the rear. If so, this bus was probably a holdout from a previous era, an old warhorse dragged from retirement to fill in on an increasingly busy route. I have an abiding memory, too, of packed buses rushing past bus stops at which frustrated commuters waited.

Between 1991 and 2011, car ownership in Ireland more than doubled. Before the advent of dedicated bus lanes and the opening of the southern section of the M50 motorway in 2001, which took large volumes of vehicular traffic away from smaller roads, it wasn't unusual to spend well over an hour – sometimes nearer two hours – travelling by bus during the morning rush from where I lived in Ballyboden to the city centre.

For my second attempt at the bus game, I decided to tweak the rules: each leg of the journey would last twenty minutes rather than ten. I thought this might bring me further from the city centre. I also wanted to minimize the chances of getting locked into a single route, and I was particularly keen to avoid the Ballybough–Marino–Malahide road corridor, so at around 11 a.m., a few days after my first trip, I walked to a bus stop on College Green, which has perhaps the densest concentration of bus routes south of the Liffey. From here buses could take me west or south-west.

The first to arrive was a number 40, going in the direction of Liffey Valley Shopping Centre. I boarded and sat downstairs, near the back. On Thomas Street, where people browsed at stalls set up along the pavement, an elderly man got on the bus and sat next to me. He held a plastic bag in his hand that smelled of fresh meat. A little while later, a woman with a small dog, a King Charles spaniel, boarded, and stood near the front doors of the bus, discussing the dog with a man sitting nearby. 'He's like a child,' she said. After twenty minutes we were in Inchicore, where I flipped a coin – needless to say, it came up tails – and crossed the road to the opposite stop, in front of a red-brick terrace just outside Richmond Park football ground. The bus that brought me back to the city centre was a 13 – a different route from the one that had brought me to Inchicore, although it followed the same streets back to the centre of the city. After twenty minutes I disembarked in O'Connell Street. A horse and cart full of bric-a-brac – rusty sewing machines, park benches – made its way up the street as cars whizzed past it, advertising a well-known tourist pub situated in the Dublin Mountains. I flipped a coin, turned up tails yet again, and crossed the wide thoroughfare to the bus stop outside the Savoy cinema.

It was now lunchtime, and Dublin's traffic was congealing. Stern choral music emerged from a small religious shop next to the cinema, one which regularly posted graphic anti-abortion material in its front window. After a few minutes a number 9 bus came along and I jumped on. It sat in traffic on O'Connell Street for the next ten minutes. By the time it had squeezed down Dame Street and turned south, my twenty minutes were nearly up. I got as far as South Circular Road before ringing the bell.

I flipped a coin – tails – and got the next number 9 back into town, where on ninety minutes I disembarked at a stop almost directly across from where I had begun my journey.

My tweaks to the game – starting from a different place, lengthening the time limit before I disembarked each bus – had not altered the basic dynamic. I had conceived the game as something that would bring an element of play into using Dublin buses but, instead of the lightness and exhilaration I had hoped for, I was feeling the extreme frustration familiar to the demoralized commuter. I had to remind myself that I didn't have to get anywhere, that I had undertaken this game of my own free will and that I could stop at any time. But I didn't want to stop, not yet. I would try again. Perhaps the game was not intrinsically mis-designed; perhaps I'd just been unlucky with the coin-flips.

I decided to revert to ten-minute journeys and, for the third attempt, a couple of weeks later, I chose to start a new trip from the stop outside Pizza Hut on Suffolk Street. This was the stop at which I would regularly disembark when getting a 15B from my parents' house to the city centre. As I had arrived on a 15B, I chose to get off here, and waited for the next bus; soon, a 39A arrived. The 39A ran along a recently extended and fairly insane 26-kilometre route from UCD to Ongar, a pastel-shaded new town that had been constructed on a former stud farm on the border between Dublin and Meath. The bus took me along the south quays, crossing the Liffey at the

James Joyce Bridge, which spans the river next to the house at 15 Usher's Island, in which Joyce's story 'The Dead' is set. The traffic along the quays had been sluggish, and by that point my ten minutes on the bus were almost up. Once the bus had crossed the river, I rang the bell and jumped out at a stop on Blackhall Place – tails yet again. I crossed the road and got another 39A heading back towards town. The day was grey and threatening rain, and the traffic edged slowly along the north quay – there had already been a significant downpour that morning. The bus swung across O'Connell Bridge to the south, and I disembarked at College Street.

The traffic had been bad all morning, and I noticed that delivery trucks, which usually would have concluded their runs by then, were still to be seen around the city unloading their cargos. Lots of things felt out of place, slightly off. Before catching the bus to Blackhall Place I had noticed queues outside several branches of Allied Irish Bank that were evidently still shut. It was almost eleven in the morning – the branches should already have been open for close to an hour. On the way to the city centre I had seen another branch of AIB with a queue waiting outside – again, it should have been open by then. Could they have been closed for training, or was there a problem with the computer systems? There had also been rumblings of possible strike action because of pay cuts, yet no strike had been declared. The queues outside banks had combined with the recent rain and heavy traffic to create the impression of a city slowing down, on the brink of systems failure. But this could have been my own projection, facing as I was another hour and a half on slow buses.

At College Street I took a 15B south, bringing me around St Stephen's Green and past the National Concert Hall, jumping off after ten minutes at South Richmond Street, where – tails again! – I crossed the road and took a 15A back in the direction of town. I climbed the stairs and saw that I was the only passenger on the upper deck.

My ninety minutes were ticking away. Tails – I arrived at Suffolk Street, and crossed to a stop on Lower Grafton Street. I climbed on to a number 4, which weaved its way east towards Merrion Square, over the Grand Canal and out towards Ballsbridge, where my ninety-minute journey ticked to a close. Tails again: I made my way across the road to the inbound bus stop, and was standing there when my stopwatch ticked past ninety minutes. I stood to let a bus pass by, one that, according to the rules, I couldn't catch.

The last vestiges of Dublin's tram system had been gone for over forty years before the two new Luas lines opened in the mid-2000s. The red line stretches from Tallaght and Saggart in south-west Dublin to the Point Depot on the north quays, while the green line runs from Bride's Glen in the south-eastern suburbs to its terminus at St Stephen's Green. While the red line runs wholly along a new route, the green line utilizes a long-defunct suburban railway line. The lines don't meet, although this will be remedied by an extension of the green line across the city centre that is due to be running in 2017. The Luas trams are sleek, silver and extremely quiet, aside from a low rumble, which is why they're equipped with two warning noises: a high-pitched bell as a general alert to pedestrians and a much louder horn that's typically used by drivers when a person or car is directly in the way of the tram.

In the economic chaos that followed the crash in the property market, it was tempting to think of Ireland as less a nation than a smoking hole in the ground. I never expected actually to locate that smoking hole in the ground, but when I travelled to Bride's Glen on the Luas green line I found a hollowed-out landscape at the terminus that seemed to embody the despair and ruination brought about by the crash. The tramway extended along a concrete viaduct above a vast crater of grey, gravelly earth. The landscape looked grim, bare, uninhabitable – as if it had been constructed using stage directions from a Samuel Beckett play. A half-built office park teetered on the eastern rim of the crater. At the end of the viaduct, just before it met a blocked-off road, was a wooden-clad cube containing two toilets used by tram drivers. I turned left, towards the office park, which looked like any other unfinished suburban business zone but was sprinkled with the dust blowing from the hole in the ground.

Just before arriving at Bride's Glen, the tram had passed through a rural scene. The Luas station at

Laughanstown seemed like a sleepy railway halt in the middle of nowhere: it was situated on a narrow country lane and appeared to have been constructed in anticipation of a residential area that hadn't yet been built. Beyond Laughanstown, a ruined medieval church stood on a ridge above open fields. This rustic landscape was more like what Beckett would have seen as he travelled on the old railway line between his family's substantial home in Foxrock and the terminus on Harcourt Street.

In 1915, aged nine, Beckett was sent to a school called Earlsfort House, which was based in a building on Adelaide Road, just a couple of minutes' walk from Harcourt Street station. The young Beckett commuted daily to school by train; later, as a student and then as a lecturer in Trinity College, he made the same trip.

The line had opened in 1854, initially running to a temporary terminus on Harcourt Road. The Harcourt Street terminal, with its distinctive stone façade of Doric columns and a central arch, still stands. What was perhaps most surprising about such an impressive-looking construction was that the station itself was so small: a single platform, with a turntable at the northern end to allow engines to change direction. On St Valentine's Day in 1900 a cattle train from Enniscorthy crashed through the wall of the station on to Hatch Street; the 22-year-old driver had misjudged the incline.

The time Beckett spent travelling along the line made an enduring impression on him. In 1924, in an article for the *Evening Telegraph*, he wrote of the apparent futility of rolling-stock manoeuvres at the station: 'incoming and outgoing trains have to play at "Box and Cox" [taking turns] perpetually. On most occasions indeed, it is truer to say that trains come in merely to go out again.' Beckett left Dublin for Paris in 1937, and returned to the city of his birth only sporadically; but Dublin's landscape continued to figure in his writings, including many obvious references to the Harcourt Street line. His radio play *All That Fall* appears to be set in Foxrock station: the allusions to a nearby racecourse suggest that of Leopardstown, which the station adjoined; the stationmaster is named Mr Barrell, which seems a nod to Thomas Farrell, the Foxrock stationmaster, with whom Beckett would have been familiar. Farrell was justifiably proud of his station, which regularly won awards for best-kept station on the line – its tidiness is ridiculed by a character in *All That Fall*. Farrell is again referenced in Beckett's novel *Watt*, where he is renamed Mr Gorman. In one passage Mr Gorman sells a ticket to Watt, while a bystander asks which end of the line Watt wishes to go to: 'the round end or the square end?' – the 'round end' being the one with the turntable, at Harcourt Street.

In Beckett's 1976 play *That Time*, three disembodied voices, speaking in an unpunctuated stream of consciousness, recall a return to the city, pointing out with regret the ways in which the place has changed – 'no trams then all gone long ago' – while remembering locations of personal significance, including the Harcourt Street terminus: 'so foot it up in the end to the station bowed half double get out to it that way all closed down and boarded up Doric terminus of the Great Southern and Eastern all closed down and the colonnade crumbling away so what next'.

The bleakness of the office park that stood on the edge of the crater at Bride's Glen stirred in me a momentary despair: there was nowhere to go and nothing to do. As I turned around to walk back towards the Luas terminus, some dust blew into my eyes. I closed them for a moment and angled my body forward, better to cut through the strong wind that swept down from the mountains through the giant hole in the ground. My eyes moistened with the dust, then dried with the wind. By the two toilets at the Luas stop I waited for the next tram.

Was there any way of making the bus game work – of experiencing joy and novelty on the buses? Having thrown tails twelve times in a row – an unlikely sequence that kept me tethered to the city centre – I decided to eliminate the coin-toss. After ten minutes on a bus I would get off at the next stop and, rather than cross the road to the opposite stop, I would stay where I was, boarding the next bus going in the same direction as the one I had just got off.

I stood at the stop near my house on the Ballycullen road in Firhouse, a suburb south of Tallaght, and got the first bus that came, the 49, in the direction of the city centre. (The only other bus to go from this stop was the 65B, which would have brought me along a similar route to the 49, until Terenure, where their paths diverge: the 49 turns towards Harold's Cross, while the 65B continues to the city centre through Rathmines.) Ten minutes later, I was in Terenure, a village on one of the main roads out of the city, which had once been known as Roundtown, on account of the circle of buildings that surrounded the junction of the roads to Templeogue and Walkinstown. Now, only one of those buildings remained, a curved, two-storey stone edifice that formed part of a car showroom.

At the Terenure stop, I could see on the digital information board that a number 16 would soon arrive. Terenure was once something of a hub for trams: two city services, the 15 and 16, ran from the main crossroads, and the stone sheds of the old DUTC tram yards could be seen peeking from behind the chip shop across the road. Todd Andrews – who would later, as chairman of CIÉ, preside over the closing of the Harcourt Street line and commission the report about disgruntled Dublin busmen – grew up in Terenure, and recalled the 'tram stables', as the yard was locally called, in reference to the sheds used for the horses which pulled the trams in the early years. Another line, the Dublin and Blessington Steam Tramway, ran from a yard west of the main crossroads, following a route that stretched deep into the Wicklow Mountains.

The 16 arrived. After ten minutes had elapsed I stepped off it on to the South Circular Road. The next bus was a 122. Another ten minutes later I was on Dame

Street, in the south city centre, and faced with a nightmare scenario: the next bus to arrive, the board told me, would be a 123, which ran the route that had nearly stranded me in Marino.

I wrestled again with breaking the rules, but in the end I boarded the 123 and sat upstairs among Italian students, who had packed the upper deck. I considered my options: I could stay there, let ten minutes elapse and end up in Marino or Fairview again, or I could break the rules and get off at the next stop, on O'Connell Street.

I rang the bell. I was consciously breaking the rules, but I couldn't deal with replicating an earlier journey so closely. I had been on the bus for around two minutes.

If I waited at the stop where I'd disembarked, there was a strong risk of getting another 123 and ending up bouncing around a corner of Dublin where the only bus I could get would be another 123, so again I broke the rules, moving up the road to another stop, where the 123 couldn't be boarded.

A number 4 came along, and I climbed on. It brought me north through Phibsborough, and along the Botanic Road in Glasnevin, where I disembarked. There was no digital information board, so I checked the printed timetable on the bus shelter and saw that there were two buses serving the stop: the number 4, which was scheduled to arrive every fifteen minutes, and the number 9, which kept a similar timetable. I looked back in the direction my bus had come from and saw another bus stop, which did have a digital information board. Perhaps

I could get the 4 or the 9 from there, I thought. Or maybe another bus? I was keenly aware that my time was ticking down and that it wasn't long until my ninety minutes would be up. I wanted to make the most of the last few minutes I had left, and I reckoned that if I went to the other bus stop I'd have a better chance of getting a bus sooner. Having already effected two cheats, I decided to make it three. On the digital information board I could see that an 83 would soon arrive.

The bus brought me through Glasnevin into Finglas, where it sat in traffic for several minutes before transporting me through open landscapes fringed with housing estates, landscapes that recalled the windswept place where I grew up. I was reminded that there were large stretches of the city – to the north and to the west – that I had often seen from a distance, and maybe even travelled through, but, when it came down to it, only vaguely knew.

My ninety minutes were up. I got off the bus, crossed the road to the opposite stop and put my hand in my trouser pocket to see if I still had any change.

A few months later I went back to the buses and travelled around for a few days. This time I didn't have the limitation of the ninety-minute card but instead used the Leap Card, a top-up debit card that's useable on all forms of Dublin transport. The Leap Card has a daily cap: after a certain amount of money is spent on the card in a single day, all remaining journeys are free.

One day I was out having a look around a housing estate near Blanchardstown, a suburb in north-west Dublin. It was getting late and dark clouds hung on the horizon, so I walked to a nearby bus stop and waited. It wasn't far from the terminus, and the timetable suggested a bus was due in the next few minutes.

A double-deck 38 turned up and I climbed on board, sitting upstairs about a third of the way from the back on the left-hand side, a position I had begun to take up on a lot of my journeys: it seemed a good spot from which to observe both what was happening on the top deck and whatever was to be seen outside.

As the bus travelled through the estates on the north side of the motorway, a couple got on and sat upstairs in the front seat – a man with a very loud midlands accent and a woman with tanned skin. She listened quietly as the man talked. He complained about something that had happened when he was driving down Gardiner Street in the city centre. A man had cut him off, and he ended up exchanging threats with him. Changing topics, he then discussed a 'coloured woman – very coloured' he had seen in a supermarket whose child had cried 'until she was sick'. At a bus stop a little further on, where a road running through a housing estate meets a large link road leading to the motorway, a Russian family got on, followed at another stop by two Chinese lads.

In Blanchardstown village a pair of Irish people got on and sat in the two seats in front of me. The lad was a wiry hipster with studs in his ears, wearing a green and black check shirt buttoned up to the very top, while the girl wore an army-green coat. Her hair was dyed a baby blonde and was wavy but tightened into a ponytail. When her head turned slightly I could see that she was wearing false eyelashes. There was a mellow smell of alcohol in the air once they got on, so I wasn't surprised to see her holding a bottle of wine wrapped in a scrunched-up brown-paper bag. She poured the wine into two SuperValu cardboard cups. Both the girl and the lad appeared to be in their early twenties.

As the bus progressed along Navan Road past large pubs, car showrooms and red-brick estates, I began to listen more closely to the conversation of the pair in front of me, which, at the beginning, sounded like a typical account of their respective jobs, but came to seem a lot more interesting. The girl was discussing washing and shampooing, so I assumed she worked as a hairdresser. She then said: 'It's not that long ago that people used to just wash them with a hose.'

It turned out that she was a dog groomer, and she briefly discussed the money that she made in Dublin compared with the sort of money she could earn for doing the same job in America. She talked about the different level of dog grooming that's carried out over there – how it's a much bigger industry altogether – and how her dream would be to go there and to continue her work on that much bigger stage.

As the bus moved through Phibsborough, she talked about drying the dogs – how some of them you put in a 'box dryer', which means they're in the dark during the drying and, because of the darkness and the warmth, they invariably fall asleep. She talked about doing their nails. The two of them discussed the logistics of getting a green card for entry to the States by marrying an American citizen, and what the going rate for an arrangement such as that was ($15,000, according to the lad).

They both got off the bus on Parnell Square, and the lad stood outside a hotel while the girl went inside.

At College Street I jumped from the bus and stood at the next stop along, where I could catch a 15B, the bus that would bring me to my parents' house. Once it arrived, the bus filled up with families and couples who had been in town, either shopping or at leisure.

We passed through Rathmines, where a group of teenage boys got on, all wearing the colours of Terenure College's rugby team – they'd just been to a game. They talked excitedly in loud voices, not really about the game at all but rather about the potential altercations that might have happened with opposition fans but, in the end, didn't. Then they began to talk a little about their Junior Certificate exam, for which they were preparing. They tried to calculate how long it was until the exam – one said a hundred days, another ninety-nine.

As the bus sped towards the hills on the darkening night, the passengers all drifted off, in ones and twos and threes. Soon the upper deck emptied, and it wasn't long before I, too, had reached my stop.

8. Ghosts of the New Wild West

Before it got to Tyrrelstown, my bus crossed the M50, entered an industrial estate – a barrier lifted to let it through – and passed a number of glass and concrete buildings that housed some of the big names of global tech: Creative, Symantec, Xerox. Outside PayPal's European headquarters stood three flagpoles, from which hung the Irish tricolour, the EU flag and the stars and stripes of the United States. Then the road narrowed; a bollard in its centre automatically withdrew into the tarmac and the bus passed over. On one side of the road there were fields; on the other, a large grey factory that belched out steam – a manufacturing facility for pharmaceuticals. There were no houses to be seen, just scrubland and electricity pylons on the southern horizon. This was north-west County Dublin, not far from the Meath border, and roughly as far from the city centre as Tallaght is.

After a roundabout, the bus entered a residential development. Tyrrelstown's main road – the Boulevard – was lined with three-storey yellow-brick houses. The Boulevard looped through the estate before arriving at a cluster of shops and a supermarket around a small square with a few parking spaces for cars. The bus pulled up to a stop in the square and I stepped off.

This was where, a bit before seven on the evening of Good Friday, 2 April 2010, Toyosi Shitta-Bey, a Nigerian fifteen-year-old who lived with his family in Tyrrelstown, and four of his male friends came to meet five girls who had made the bus trip from the city centre. In under two hours' time, Toyosi would be dead.

Suburbia is a purgatory that can become hell, yet its developers always sell it as heaven. Tyrrelstown was built according to principles devised specifically in order to avoid replicating the windswept, car-bound anomie that marks so much of twentieth-century suburbia.

In 1973, Essex County Council published *A Design Guide for Residential Areas*. The Essex Design Guide, as the slender book came to be known, was a reaction against the anonymous sprawl that had quickly come to characterize post-war suburbs in the UK. It described recent housing developments as 'depressingly characterless . . . wide open spaces dotted with dwarf trees' with 'anywhere-type houses . . . packaged together in a manner devoid of identity or sense of place'.

The Essex Design Guide suggested that, rather than building more sprawling estates that prioritized automobile traffic, new housing should be set in landscaped streets narrower than typical suburban roads. A housing development should have a hierarchy of streets, from the local distributor road, which would allow marginally faster traffic, right down to the private drive, which would serve a maximum of three dwellings. The design guidelines also distrusted straight lines, finding them 'psychologically exhausting'; instead, the visual length of a space 'should be limited by complete or partial closure, formed by curves in the street, changes in the building line or changes of level'.

In February 1999, Fingal Council's architect David O'Connor spoke at a housing conference about how new housing estates lacked a 'sense of place' and suggested that planners should be looking at established urban communities for inspiration. He took issue with conventional road design, querying the width of suburban roads and their high speed limits of up to 40mph. He suggested lowering the limit to 20mph on narrow, curving streets, and bringing houses closer to the street. These measures would allow building at a higher density – higher density being, in principle, conducive to livelier community and commercial life, and less car-dependency. Many of O'Connor's ideas about residential planning were in line with those Essex Council planners had drawn up in 1973.

A year after O'Connor spoke, Fingal Council granted permission to a developer called Twinlite to build over two thousand houses on a site in north-west Dublin beyond Blanchardstown, which used to be a golf course and farmers' fields. (A planning application to turn the area into a landfill had been refused in 1995.) Perhaps it is not surprising, in light of the council architect's remarks, that when preparing to build Tyrrelstown the developers recruited Melville Dunbar Associates to devise a master plan for the development. The CEO of the company, the veteran architect and planner Melville Dunbar, was the 'prime mover' of the Essex Design Guide, according to that book's acknowledgements. Although Tyrrelstown does not follow the guide's preference for semi-detached houses in a neo-vernacular style, its dense, labyrinthine streetscape shows the mark of Dunbar.

There are no straight lines in Tyrrelstown – every road curves. Even the tiniest side streets are kinked with dog-legs and chicanes. What was conceived in the Essex Design Guide as an antidote to the prairie-like characterlessness of suburbia seemed in practice merely to substitute tight corners for open space, claustrophobia for agoraphobia. While supposedly pedestrian-friendly, Tyrrelstown felt like a maze, and I found it a difficult place to navigate on foot. It lacked the linear logic I had come to expect from suburban streets.

With its numerous three- and four-storey buildings closely plotted within an area of roughly a square kilometre, Tyrrelstown's population of six thousand lives at a density almost twice the Dublin average. This makes sense in itself – in general, Dublin's population is too spread out, and the city's sprawl has a number of unpleasant social and economic consequences. But urban density is not merely a matter of people per square kilometre, and it can be difficult to replicate the dynamics of established urban areas in new-build suburbia. If Tyrrelstown represents a variety of 'urbanism', it is a very particular one, with only a single small commercial district, and surrounded by green fields and a golf course. On my visits, I couldn't help feeling much the same chill I got when I thought about the suburbs of my youth. I wondered whether this new suburb was any more conducive to human happiness than the ones I had grown up in.

A couple of days before my bus trip to Tyrrelstown, I sat on my parents' sofa and watched *Bad Day at Black Rock*, the modern Western set after the Second World War, which begins with Spencer Tracy arriving on a train in a small desert town and ends with him solving a racially motivated murder case. The memory of the film unexpectedly coloured my feelings on arrival in Tyrrelstown. Tracy, playing a one-armed war veteran, climbed from a train at an empty halt and was soon met with silence from the town's small population, who, it emerges over the course of the film, had conspired to cover up the murder. My arrival – stepping off the bus in Tyrrelstown – lacked the cinematic drama of Spencer Tracy's, and I didn't think the population of Tyrrelstown had covered anything up, and the case had never achieved full resolution: Paul Barry, the man charged with stabbing Toyosi, died in prison before he came to trial. (His brother, Michael Barry, was later acquitted of being an accessory to the killing.) But I thought I could learn something more about the death of Toyosi Shitta-Bey, by visiting the places he and his friends had been that evening.*

---

* In the absence of court transcripts, I have relied on contemporary newspaper accounts of the trial of Michael Barry in trying to piece together the movements of Toyosi and his friends and the events of the evening he was killed. I must also acknowledge the generous assistance

Although Tyrrelstown looks very different from Kilna-managh, the estate where I grew up – it's more compact, more walkable, and there is a substantial immigrant population of the sort that did not exist anywhere in Ireland when I was young – I could recognize the kind of suburban emptiness that starts out feeling exciting, a blank slate on which anything can be written, but ends up a slow boredom that you need to escape by whatever means you can. When you're a child, everything seems full of possibility. Later, you're bored and you're a teenager, and it seems like there's nothing to do except hang around, watch television and wait for something to happen, although you're pretty sure it never will.

In the square, a man in a fluorescent jacket used a telescopic pole with a cloth on one end to clean the windows of Pizza Hut Delivery. Shoppers passed by, walking in the direction of the houses and apartments to the west.

One of the girls who arrived on the bus to meet Toyosi and his friends had needed to use the toilet, so the girls went into the bathroom at the Chinese restaurant nearby. Above the glass shopfront, on the day I visited, a black sign gave the name of the restaurant – Aurora Asian Cuisine – in chrome lettering. On either side of the doorway were statues of Chinese lions which looked like they were made of metal.

While the girls were in there, the lads walked across a

of Nicola Donnelly, who covered the trial for the *Evening Herald* and shared her recollections with me.

car park to the Lidl supermarket that stands to the east of the town square. I now crossed the car park, which was about half full, and entered the supermarket. In the aisle where freshly baked items were displayed, I picked out a salted pretzel and two triple-chocolate cookies, put them in a plastic bag and walked to the till.

I strolled back towards the main square, across Lidl's car park, and continued past the shops, reaching a round-about. To my right, the way my bus had come, was the area of Tyrrelstown known as French Park. Toyosi's friend Bobby Kuti lived here, and it was here that the five lads had been watching television before they walked around the corner to meet the girls off the bus.

It was reported in a number of outlets that Toyosi and his friends had been returning that evening from the National Aquatic Centre, an indoor swimming complex four kilometres east of Tyrrelstown, when the killing took place; and this detail continued to be reported after the trial was complete. When I raised it with Nicola Donnelly, a reporter who had attended the trial, she told me that there had been no discussion there of the Aquatic Centre. It wasn't clear whether what had been reported about the Aquatic Centre was an error or – if the lads had been at the pool earlier in the day – simply an irrelevance. It seemed to me that, when a child is killed, we'd rather believe that child was coming home from a swimming pool than drifting around a housing estate.

After leaving Lidl, Toyosi and his friends walked west-ward, into the part of Tyrrelstown known as Mount

Garrett. I crossed a park, which had in it a combined basketball and five-a-side football court – the small goals
tucked at the base of the overhanging hoops – and a playground with swings, slides and a see-saw. At one end of
the basketball court, a group of black children passed
around a football, while at the other an Asian child played
basketball with his father. Parents leaned against the low
fence around the play area for younger kids, watching
their children.

Following the little wobbling roads west of the park, I
passed a small, wedge-shaped green space surrounded by
two-storey houses. A few South Asian children played outside their house. The road turned right again, and I found
myself at the Boulevard. I crossed the road and walked
anticlockwise in the direction of Mount Garrett Rise.

Adjacent to Mount Garrett Rise there is an open green
space – probably the biggest such space in Tyrrelstown,
apart from the park. In the centre of the field was a cluster of trees among which a group of children played. A
row of three-storey townhouses, gathered in terraces
whose façades were finished in yellow or red brick, curved
along the edge of the green space to the left, while to the
right were semi-detached two-storey houses finished in
similar yellow or red brick. Beyond these houses was the
western perimeter of Tyrrelstown, marked by electricity
pylons and a hedgerow behind a flimsy-looking wire
fence.

I circled around Mount Garrett Rise for a while before
I found the house I was looking for, the house where Paul

Barry had lived. Paul Barry was the 38-year-old man who was charged with stabbing Toyosi Shitta-Bey. The house faced a strip of grassland that sloped down to the base of an electricity pylon. It was on this strip that one of the girls in Toyosi's group had asked Paul Barry for a light for a cigarette. Bobby Kuti testified that Toyosi had told him he believed he had already met Paul Barry at his football club – Toyosi was a youth player for Shelbourne FC – and that he believed him to be a racist.

After this, according to the prosecuting counsel, a verbal row erupted. Two neighbours told the court that they heard racist shouts. According to the transcript of his interview with gardaí on the night of Toyosi's death, Paul Barry's brother Michael, then aged twenty-three, had been sitting in his jeep, trying to work the GPS system on his phone, when the row started. He saw the group confronting his brother, got out of the car and walked towards them. According to the transcript read in court, he claimed that he was a member of the gardaí and asked them to move on, but they laughed at him. Bobbi Kuti testified that he threw the first punch at Paul Barry, thinking that he was about to attack him. Michael Barry moved between the group and his brother; his hand was kicked and he dropped his mobile phone; Kuti testified that the phone was picked up by Toyosi. Michael Barry fell to the ground. Kuti testified that he and the four other lads were 'swinging' at the Barry brothers. Michael Barry said that, while on the ground, he was kicked in the ribs, while an eyewitness testified that Paul

Barry was also kicked when on the ground. Michael Barry said that he threw a punch at the male black teen who was kicking his brother. According to the prosecution, the fight ended when a baseball bat was produced from Paul Barry's house. At that point, the kids fled. At the trial, Bobby Kuti testified that they had laughed because they were relieved: 'We were kids at the time and thought the row was all over then.' He believed that they 'didn't have to worry any more'.

Paul and Michael Barry got into the black jeep and went in search of Toyosi and his friends. Michael Barry told gardaí on the night of the killing that he wasn't aware that his brother had a knife with him; they merely wanted to 'grab one to see if he had my phone'. The Barrys found the kids near a roundabout west of the playground.

One of Toyosi's friends, Gracia Lulendo, testified that Paul Barry got out of the passenger side of the jeep and walked towards him, holding the knife in his right hand and saying, 'Come on, you nigger.' Lulendo, who said he was in shock, picked up a branch to defend himself. Toyosi, seeing his friend was in trouble, stepped in between them and was stabbed once in the chest. He ran before falling to the ground.

At 9.05 p.m., when he was admitted to the James Connolly Memorial Hospital in Blanchardstown, Toyosi Shitta-Bey was pronounced dead. An ambulance crew had attempted to revive him at the scene, but he had lost a lot of blood very quickly. According to the coroner, the knife caused 'a single stab wound to the left upper chest measuring 3.6cm by 2cm and 13cm in depth'.

Neither the knife nor Michael Barry's mobile phone was ever found.

From Mount Garrett Rise, I returned to the Boulevard and continued anticlockwise for a couple of minutes to the roundabout near which Toyosi died. Beyond it, there are a couple of speed bumps in the road, and next to the speed bumps is a lamp post, numbered '52'. Photos of the scene from the night of the killing show a blue tent erected here to shield the crime scene from view. After Toyosi died, flowers were left at the lamp post and tributes taped to it.

On 6 April, four days after Toyosi's death, Paul Barry was charged with manslaughter, while Michael Barry was charged under section 11 of the Firearms and Offensive Weapons Act. In September 2010, both charges were upgraded to murder. In November 2011, just before the case was due to come to trial, Paul Barry was found dead in his jail cell. Michael Barry was tried in December 2012. After a few days, the judge directed the jury to find him not guilty, in the absence of any evidence that he knew his brother was carrying a knife when they left Mount Garrett Rise.

The stabbing of Toyosi Shitta-Bey was quickly interpreted as racially motivated. Gardaí and local politicians, while unwilling to deny a racial factor, appealed for calm until more was known. A movement grew to express solidarity with Toyosi's bereaved family, and on Easter Monday, three days after the killing, a vigil was held in Tyrrelstown. A few days later a demonstration was held in Dublin city centre at which a largely African and Irish crowd commemorated Toyosi. A representative of the Shitta-Bey family addressed the demonstration, as did socialist politician Joe Higgins and Jack O'Connor, the president of SIPTU, Ireland's largest trade union. All the speeches expressed a desire that peaceful integration be achieved in Ireland and that Toyosi's death would not be in vain. Higgins, at the time a member of the European Parliament, was keen to reassure *Irish Times* journalist Kathy Sheridan that 'Tyrrelstown is not like Watts County, waiting to explode' – a reference to the six-day riot that took place in Los Angeles in 1965 during which African-American residents protested against deprivation and police brutality and over a thousand buildings were damaged or burned.

Soon after Toyosi's death, Mary White, the Minister of State for Equality, and Human Rights and Integration, said she had no doubt that there were 'pockets of Ireland where racism rears its ugly head'. She said that she would speak out about racism in Ireland, and that she would travel around the country talking to immigrants: 'I am a good listener, I want to hear their voices.' She spoke of setting up a new ministerial council on integration, an integration taskforce for the delivery of services to immigrants and a third body, made up of academic and Civil Service appointments. She later hinted at a system of monitoring racist incidents in Ireland that would not involve reporting them to the gardaí, saying that it was 'something innovative that has not been tried before'. These hints and plans didn't seem to yield tangible results. After the General Election in 2011, the minister of state's portfolio was combined with portfolios for mental health and disability and the word 'integration' removed from the title. This change was perceived as a downgrade by the Migrant Rights Centre Ireland, which voiced its concern about the lack of a specific minister responsible for integration. There's now a website for an Office for the Promotion of Migrant Integration which is updated sporadically, and on the contact page I found an old email address listed, beside which was written in red: 'DO NOT USE'. It offers an alternative contact address, but the persistence of the old one is indicative of the much-diminished status of integration policy.

Ireland, with its had a long history of emigration to other countries, seemed much less surefooted when addressing the relatively new phenomenon of inward migration. When I asked Dr Mary Gilmartin, a geography lecturer from the National University of Ireland, Maynooth, who has researched immigration patterns in Ireland, whether the Irish state was sufficiently committed to integration policies, she was wholly unambiguous in her answer: 'The Irish state has no integration policies. It only has a statement on integration management' – the cheerily titled 'Migration Nation', a large-print document published in 2008 that proceeded from the assumption that Ireland's history of emigration would uniquely equip the nation for the challenges of inward migration. Dr Gilmartin cited the loss of a minister with specific responsibility for integration, along with cuts in funding to language support and poor representation of minorities in public bodies as indicative of this lack of commitment.

A few months before I travelled by bus to Tyrrelstown to retrace the path Toyosi and his friends took on the day he was killed, I met Nuala Kane, a community coordinator with the Blanchardstown Area Partnership, at her office in Parslickstown House, an old two-storey stone building that's been extended at the rear to accommodate office and classroom space. Nuala's catchment area runs from Mulhuddart village as far north as Tyrrelstown, and I wanted to talk to her about life in the north-western sub-urbs, including the question of immigrant integration. Parslickstown House was owned by the council and housed a number of community projects, and I sat with Nuala, who lived in a council estate near Blanchardstown shopping centre, at a table outside the building as she told me about the area and its development.

When Parslickstown House was acquired by the council in the early 1990s, it was on the far western edge of the Mulhuddart area and in extremely poor condition. The Blanchardstown shopping centre, a huge commer-cial development across the motorway from Mulhuddart, didn't yet exist. Over the years, the house was improved, and business units were established in old farming buildings on the site. While I was there, people arrived for courses or sat in the downstairs café. Meanwhile, traffic for the business units came and went via the on-site car park.

I asked Nuala about the way the area was perceived and mentioned the death of Toyosi Shitta-Bey. She interrupted me, addressing my question only indirectly: 'See, good news doesn't sell newspapers.' But she went on to talk about tension between immigrants and natives in the area. She mentioned an incident in which ten African families, who were on the council's housing list, were moved into newly built houses on a council estate. Residents of the estate, some of whom had relatives on the housing list and had expected them to be given priority for the new housing, were angered by this. The council explained that the African families were next on the housing list, and thus entitled to take up the housing. The locals wanted to be pushed to the top of the queue on the basis of their residency in the area, and were primed to query anything which they thought resembled favouritism towards the Africans, and they reacted violently. 'What we heard as community workers was the ten [African] families were all sleeping in the one house at night because the houses were being attacked and they were afraid of their life,' Nuala said. She felt that the council could have handled the situation better by holding meetings and informing the residents of what was happening.

I told her about how I had contacted the press office of the Garda Síochána asking to discuss issues of integration and community policing. They had responded by saying they couldn't help me. Nuala gave me the number of a community police officer. I spoke to him by phone, and he promised to meet me, but I never heard from him again. I later rang the Garda Racial, Intercultural and Diversity Office, who told me that I would have to go through the press office before talking to them officially. Although Nuala spoke highly of the effectiveness of community policing in the area, I was left with serious doubts about the police force's commitment to openness. I was a freelance writer, not someone who could pose a threat to the gardaí in the newspapers or on television – perhaps they didn't think I was worth bothering with.

The first big wave of the Dublin suburbs' westward expansion started in the 1960s, with the development of extensive new estates in Tallaght, Clondalkin, Lucan and Blanchardstown. The construction of Tyrrelstown was part of a more recent wave that also included Citywest, Ongar and Adamstown. One day I decided to have a look around Adamstown, a development of apartments and houses located along a main railway line near Lucan. Coming from the direction of Tallaght, I cycled down a lane adjoining a broad dual carriageway that marked the western extent of south

Dublin and linked Tallaght with Lucan. Once you reached Lucan, it wasn't far across the River Liffey to Blanchardstown and Tyrrelstown.

Nearing Adamstown, I passed a recently built railway station that hadn't opened – concrete barriers prevented entry to the building, and I could see staircases and lift shafts leading down to the empty platforms. This was to be Kishoge station, a suburban stop on the railway line leading west from Dublin's Heuston station. It was meant to serve a development called Clonburris, which was to occupy a 700-acre strip of land south of the railway line and north of the Grand Canal. But Clonburris was never built, and the 700 acres are still agricultural fields. An official website promoting Clonburris, dating from 2008, notes that the new development was to be based on the 'Adamstown model'.

I turned left, and followed an interminably long road that led westwards alongside the railway line. Sweeping past a Centra that appeared to be the only open shop unit nearby, I continued towards Adamstown's railway station. To my right, neat three- and four-storey yellow-brick apartment buildings surrounded two nearly identical school buildings: a secondary school run by the County Dublin Vocational Education Committee and a non-denominational primary school. (Around the corner, there's a Catholic primary school.) Near the bus terminus there was a sheltered line of bike stands at which not a single bike was parked. Along the right side of the road was a long black wooden hoarding on which were draped purple banners bearing slogans such as 'Your Kind of Town' and 'Home for Good'. The hoardings shielded a vast stretch of undeveloped ground from view. The station building consisted of a wide bridge across the tracks sheltered by glass and a rubberized canopy stretched across a metal frame. There was a steady traffic of trains passing through or stopping but, at that point in the afternoon, a little before rush hour, there were no passengers to be seen. A taxi rank was marked out on the road, but it wasn't clear if it had ever been used by taxis; instead, people parked their cars there.

Through a gap in the wooden hoarding on the other side of the road I saw a large field that had gone to seed. On the horizon was a four-storey glass building whose coloured internal dividing walls were clearly visible – an indication of its emptiness. Where there might have been desks and coat racks and pinboards and computer workstations and filing cabinets there were nothing but colours – bright green, mustard yellow, burnt orange, purple, powder blue – bouncing through the glass across the empty landscape.

Adamstown wasn't quite a ghost estate – those unoccupied housing developments on the fringes of Irish towns that became internationally recognized icons of Ireland's economic folly. Some of it is finished and occupied. But it is hard not to be mesmerized by the scale of what has not been finished. When I cycled east between more wooden hoardings and past a fully developed stretch of apartments, I got a sense of what Adamstown might have been like had it been completed. Elegant four-storey apartment blocks, finished in yellow brick, glass and wood panelling, extended on either side of a moderately wide two-lane avenue along which rows of trees lined the broad footpaths. In the network of streets on either side of the main road were smaller buildings: apartments of three storeys and terraces of red-brick houses. Adamstown had been carefully planned by South Dublin County Council – a process which included input from anyone who expressed an interest, including prospective residents. It wasn't conceived merely as an estate – it was to be a complete new town. Even the place name, which was drawn from a local townland, evoked Edenic possibilities: the word 'Adamstown', one planner wrote, was 'felt to envision a new beginning, the creation of something different and distinctive'.

The construction of Dublin's modern suburbs was heavily shaped by bad planning, which was enabled by political corruption. The expansion of the suburbs was generally led by developers, and bribery was rife: a speculator could make a huge amount of money if land they owned was re-zoned for residential, commercial or industrial use. In Frank McDonald and Kathy Sheridan's *The Builders*, the authors cite the figure of Fianna Fáil's Ray Burke as a perfect illustration of this tendency. In 1974, it was reported that, for his part in the re-zoning of land near Swords in north County Dublin, he received £15,000 from a company controlled by the developers Brennan and

McGowan – the same builders who had during the same period constructed Kilnamanagh, the estate on which I grew up. It later turned out that they had also built Burke's house, for free. While the planning staff of Dublin County Council objected to the development of the site, councillors voted in favour of the re-zoning. Such corrupt practices persisted during the late twentieth century, an era in which Dublin's suburbs expanded rapidly – and were stubbornly ignored by government. In the 1990s, a developer's agent, speaking anonymously to the *Irish Times*, called certain councillors 'power brokers' who 'put a value on their votes'.

Responding to an anonymous call in 1995 for tip-offs about re-zoning corruption, James Gogarty, the former managing director of the engineering firm JMSE Ltd, alleged that in June 1989 he had seen the handing over of brown envelopes that contained a total of £80,000 to Ray Burke, who at the time held two ministerial portfolios in the Fianna Fáil–Progressive Democrat coalition government. The money was paid by JMSE and a developer called Bovale to help ease planning difficulties for a number of sites in north Dublin. Politicians from all the main parties resisted any inquiry into these allegations. In July 1997, just after Burke had been appointed Minister for Foreign Affairs in the newly elected Fianna Fáil government, a series of allegations were made about his corrupt practices and the current-affairs magazine *Magill* published a letter in which Bovale's Mick Bailey told James Gogarty that he could 'procure' a majority of

Dublin County Council to support the re-zoning of land owned by JMSE. In October 1997, Burke resigned from the Dáil and the government established a tribunal of inquiry into allegations of planning corruption. This tribunal revealed that £112,000 had been paid by developer Owen O'Callaghan to fifteen councillors to secure their votes for the re-zoning of 180 acres of land at Quarryvale in west Dublin. The money was handed out to councillors in car parks, hotels and pubs by Frank Dunlop, a political lobbyist. This land subsequently became the site of the Liffey Valley Shopping Centre. During the late 1990s and early 2000s, as property became more and more central to the Irish economy, the links between developers and politicians became less furtive and increasingly blatant – notably, the Fianna Fáil tent at the Galway Races, where developers and businessmen paid €4,000 for a table of ten in 2006, the tent making around €250,000 for the party in a week.

Needless to say, such flawed planning processes weren't conducive to the creation of pleasant suburbs. Adamstown was, in part, an effort to create a blueprint led by the public interest rather than by developers. In the mid-1990s, developer Joe O'Reilly's Castlethorn Construction had bought three hundred acres of land around Adamstown, expecting that, due to its proximity to the Dublin to Cork railway line, it would be re-zoned for residential development. Sure enough, in the 1998 South Dublin County Development Plan, the lands at Adamstown were zoned as residential. In June 2001, Adamstown was designated Ireland's first Strategic Development Zone (SDZ) – a type of scheme that accelerated the planning process with the aim of delivering new homes quickly. In 2001, South Dublin County Council developed a Local Area Plan, then in December 2002 published a draft planning scheme for Adamstown. After submissions and subsequent changes, this was adopted in May 2003. By June 2004, Castlethorn had submitted the first planning application and, in September, SDCC granted planning permission for 407 dwelling units, including 77 social and affordable units, on a ten-hectare site. In February 2005, the first sod was turned on the site, and by February 2006 the initial phase of housing launched. Adamstown aimed to provide high-density housing within walking distance of amenities and with easy access to public transport, both rail and bus. The emphasis was on creating a streetscape – a network of streets, squares and public spaces – that ran through the development, rather than a mere network of roads. Provision of facilities would happen in phases as the building of houses progressed. There were to be thirteen phases in all, the first consisting of a thousand units, and each subsequent phase consisting of eight hundred units. The eventual population of Adamstown was projected to be thirty thousand.

A few days after my first trip to Adamstown, I phoned a resident of the development, Tom Dowling, who told me about his own part in its evolution. In 1998, when the lands at Adamstown were first being re-zoned, the nearby suburb of Lucan, where Dowling lived at the time, was expanding at a rapid rate – between 1996 and 2002 it almost doubled in population, to just over thirty thousand people. This expansion mostly consisted of private housing estates of semi-detached homes – a familiar Dublin suburban form whose low density has a consequent impact on traffic and the provision of services: shops and other facilities are thinner on the ground and further away, and most trips are taken by car. When the development of Adamstown was mooted, Lucan residents thought that building a new town of thirty thousand people, effectively doubling the population of the area, would be 'just mad if it's not going to be developed properly', Dowling told me. He helped form a residents' group which focused on Adamstown being as well planned as possible. 'We weren't against the development of houses, we weren't against the development of apartments, we weren't against anything really, as long as it was done properly and that it built a proper community, not just a housing development,' he said.

The first houses in Adamstown were sold in early 2006, and the train station opened the following year. By that point, Dublin house prices were at their peak. The development of amenities in Adamstown, such as a park, a swimming pool and a commercial centre, was tied to the development of houses in blocks of four hundred or eight hundred. 'So each time the developer built four hundred houses or eight hundred houses, there were key infrastructural pieces that came with that development. They couldn't go on to the 401st house or the 801st house until that key piece of infrastructure was there.' But when the bottom fell out of the market, development stopped, and further infrastructure, such as a civic centre, wasn't built. Now, South Dublin County Council was holding consultations on what should be done with the undeveloped land. Dowling felt that the council and the developer were pushing for the construction of lower-density housing that was more likely to sell; he felt this was also a way of the developer getting around its commitment to the provision of amenities.

Of the 10,000 units originally envisaged, 1,400 had been built and 1,249 had been occupied by December 2012. The yawning vastness of the void – the sheer volume of negative space left by the undeveloped stretches of waste ground – dwarfed the inhabited sections of the site, making the houses feel huddled together on the frontier of a dark and impenetrable wilderness.

On my second visit to Adamstown, I cycled through back roads and laneways that Dowling had told me about. I slipped down an alleyway that ran between two large buildings and led to a small, neat green space adjoining the area behind one of the schools. I continued along a path which led across the green space and joined Adamstown Avenue, a broad main street with bus lanes running in both directions. Four-storey apartment blocks built in red and yellow brick flanked the road. Their windows were large and square and, aside from the entry doors for staircases leading to upper storeys, there were also separate front doors providing access to what I assumed to be duplex street-level apartments. But as I cycled west along the main street, the buildings thinned out and were replaced with painted wooden barriers running along on either side of the road. Just visible beyond the barrier to my right was an unfinished building: scaffolding poked above the barrier, and I hazarded a guess that the ground floor might have been near completion. Nevertheless, the site was now deserted. As I went onwards, the railway station came into view to my left, separated from me by a wooden fence and hundreds of metres of disused ground. My journey was dragging me almost magnetically towards the chasm of empty space. Stranded beyond the fence was the colourful but empty building I had noted on my earlier trip. I considered what Adamstown would look like if the street extended beyond that fence, if there were a park behind it rather than waste ground, and what it would look like if that fence weren't there at all. It formed a physical border between the mostly developed part of Adamstown and what lay undeveloped, the border between a compromised past and an uncertain future.

At the end of my walk around Tyrrelstown, having retraced the journey Toyosi Shitta-Bey and his friends took that Good Friday night, I returned to the town square and sat down on a bench. I thought about the lamp post that stands near the spot where Toyosi was stabbed, and how there was nothing to tell you about what had occurred there – no dead flowers, no tattered photos taped to its metal casing. In the aftermath of Toyosi's death, hundreds of people had gathered on the streets of Tyrrelstown, hundreds more attended demonstrations against racism in the city centre and politicians promised to make integration a priority. I wondered what I had expected from the place where a young man had died senselessly on a night that he and his friends went walking just because they were looking for something to do. Was all that now forgotten?

I later learned that there is a memorial to Toyosi Shitta-Bey in Tyrrelstown. By the all-weather pitch near the playground in the park is a rough-hewn piece of granite that's smooth and polished on one side. On the smooth side of the stone there's an oval-shaped photo of Toyosi, below which are his name, his dates of birth and death and a few lines in memory of him, embossed in gold letters on a rectangular piece of black marble attached to the stone. The memorial was placed there in 2013, and its presence didn't go unnoticed: objections against it were lodged with the council. One objector, who spoke to the *Evening Herald*, said she found the memorial 'very distressing' and that 'the council had no right to put that where children play'.

9. Ballsbridge, Ghost Town

I started with a coffee at the dark wooden bar of Doheny & Nesbitt, a public house on Baggot Street whose supposed centrality to the fortunes of the Irish economy has, over the decades, become axiomatic and self-reinforcing. In the 1980s, when a nexus of economists and politicians conceived a new path for Ireland – lower taxation, reduced import duties and the active cultivation of foreign investment – journalists started to refer to the 'Doheny & Nesbitt school of economics'. A *New York Times* article published in January 2009 recorded the following scene: the property developer Seán Dunne, after an evening of champagne cocktails and Guinness in Doheny's, retrieving a penny from the pub's floor, before telling the journalist that he wasn't too proud to do so, and that he knew the value of money. Whether he knew the value of money or not, Seán Dunne, like most of the big Irish developers, was bust.

Nothing era-defining seemed to be going on in Doheny & Nesbitt's, so I finished my coffee and headed out, turning left.

Baggot Street describes a crooked line between government and privilege: it runs roughly south-westward from near Government Buildings on Merrion Street in the direction of Ballsbridge, arguably Dublin's wealthiest district. I passed the former offices of the *Sunday Tribune*, which had been founded in 1980 but ceased publication in 2011, following a decline in circulation. A little further on, I paused at the steps of the former Bank of Ireland headquarters, a striking bronze-tinted modernist office building built in the 1970s. The bank had sold the building for €212 million in 2006 – a peak-of-the-market offload that might have indicated that it anticipated the bad times coming and was taking prudent measures to ease the pain. But soon Bank of Ireland, like all the other banks, would require rescuing by the state. In December 2012, the old headquarters building was bought by the family of beef baron Larry Goodman; although the price paid is unknown, the guide price was €30–35 million.

The building had once been a flashpoint for preservationists: to make way for its construction, a row of red-brick Georgian houses had been demolished at 5 a.m. one Sunday in 1973. Many similar houses in the area were now listed as protected structures. (For its part, the Bank of Ireland building is now regarded as a rare example of high-quality architectural modernism in central Dublin, and itself became listed in 2006.) During the boom, banks had shovelled cash into the hands of developers, given homebuyers 100 per cent mortgages and allowed 'self-certification' on the part of borrowers. I remembered taking a small loan from my bank in

2008 and being surprised, as I read the application form, to see that I didn't have to provide any proof of income.

As you head out of town, Baggot Street becomes Pembroke Road. On the triangular traffic island where it dovetails with Northumberland Road is a tiny octagonal kiosk with terracotta roof tiles and 37 square feet of floor space. A brief account of the kiosk's history provides a small insight into the cost of commercial property in Ballsbridge. It was built in 1920. In 1989, when it was still a newspaper kiosk, it changed hands for £132,000 and thus became the most expensive piece of real estate, per square foot, ever sold in Ireland. It was sold again, for a small profit, in 1998, and put on the market once more in 2013. When I passed it, it was occupied by an independent coffee company that sold an extremely rare brew whose beans had passed through the digestive system of the Asian palm civet, a furry, cat-like, tree-dwelling creature. Years after the property crash had put a damper on many of the strange habits of Dublin consumers, a 250-gramme bag of the coffee could be bought at the kiosk for €150.

Immediately across from the kiosk is the site where Seán Dunne wanted to build his tower.

Seán Dunne's story – usefully told by Frank McDonald and Kathy Sheridan in *The Builders* – is the old one, almost a cliché among the big developers of the boom: he grew up with nothing. In a radio interview in 2008 he stressed his humble origins: he was born in Tullow in County Carlow in 1954, one of five children, and from the age of twelve he worked 'making hay, thinning beet, picking potatoes . . . on building sites'. He qualified as a quantity surveyor, then spent two years working in Canada on the extraction of oil from tar sands. Returning to Dublin, he got a job overseeing the building of local-authority houses at Jobstown in Tallaght. Subsequently he started his own construction firm, specializing in social housing. During the 1980s he spent some time working in London, before returning in 1989 to Dublin. He joined a consortium that bought St Helen's, an eighteenth-century house on seventy acres in Booterstown, for £17.75 million, built apartments in the grounds and developed the house as a hotel. As the market heated up, Dunne began flipping buildings for a quick profit and buying up sites for future development: office buildings in Dublin city centre and pockets of land on the city's fringes, such as Woodtown Manor on Stocking Lane, which he bought from the Guinness heir Garech Browne for £1.4 million in 1997. By 2005, according to Frank McDonald and Kathy Sheridan, the site was reputedly worth more than €250 million.

In the boom years Dunne resembled a well-groomed barman who had won the lottery but turned up for shifts just in case it all went wrong: short silver hair, shirt, tie, waistcoat, jacket, cufflinks and a permanent scowl that he occasionally forced into a cynical smile. A photo taken in 2008 at Punchestown Races shows a tweed-clad Dunne grinning alongside his wife, the gossip columnist Gayle Killilea, and Bertie Ahern, who would resign as

Taoiseach a couple of weeks later. In 2002 Dunne had met Killilea in the Fianna Fáil tent at Galway Races, a notorious site of networking for political and business elites. In 2004 they were married, on a yacht once owned by Aristotle Onassis which had been bought and refurbished by a group of Irish businessmen.

Just after Fianna Fáil was elected to government in 1997, the developer donated £80,250 to the party, which remained in power until 2011. In 2002, Dunne flew Ahern to Cardiff for the Heineken Cup final. Dunne and his wife were Ahern's guests at the Taoiseach's address to the UK Houses of Parliament in May 2007, and again when he addressed the US Congress in April 2008.

By then, Dunne was the embattled owner of a massive chunk of Ballsbridge.

He had started, in the summer of 2005, by purchasing Jurys Hotel and Towers, directly opposite the Pembroke Road kiosk, for €260 million. At €53.7 million per acre, it was by a distance the most expensive piece of property ever sold in Dublin to that point. Shortly thereafter, Dunne bought the adjacent Berkeley Court Hotel, on Lansdowne Road, for €57.5 million per acre. Calculations of the price per acre were not merely academic. Dunne was not interested in the hotels: he was interested in the land they sat on. He was not the only one. The next property to be sold in the suddenly red-hot Pembroke Road–Lansdowne Road–Shelbourne Road triangle was the former UCD Veterinary College, bought in November 2005 by the developer Ray Grehan at a new record price of over €81 million per acre. And, in August 2006, Dunne acquired Hume House, a 1960s office building on two thirds of an acre beside Jurys, by swapping a new and much larger office building on Sir John Rogerson's Quay in the docklands. McDonald and Sheridan write, 'the swap deal was estimated to be worth €130 million, which meant the price on the Ballsbridge site equated to an all-time record of €195 million per acre'.

Dunne quickly announced ambitious plans for the vast site he now owned. Images produced to illustrate the buildings' relationship with the surrounding area showed an angular glass-clad structure of thirty-two storeys. (The tower grew to thirty-seven storeys in the plans submitted to the city council.) There were also to be seven other buildings between ten and eighteen storeys in height.

Dublin possesses few genuinely tall buildings, and those that do exist are perennially under threat: the concrete towers at Ballymun were for the most part razed between 2004 and 2008, while the owners of the tallest building in central Dublin, the sixteen-storey Liberty Hall, have petitioned to have it knocked down and replaced. During the boom years, the logic of building higher in Dublin was clear: as an antidote to the city's sprawl, and to help satisfy the demand for office space in the city centre; but the local authorities were ambivalent about high-rise development, and little was actually built. In January 2008, Dublin City Council published a policy document entitled 'Maximising the City's Potential: A Strategy for Intensification and Height'. The council document pinpointed districts around the city as potential zones of higher-density development. But Ballsbridge was not one of the named locales, and when, in March 2008, the council granted planning permission for a number of elements of Dunne's scheme, it refused permission for the highest tower. The council's report cited the 'lack of sufficient policy support for a building of 37 storeys' – it contravened a development plan that had been in place since 2005.

Having fiercely opposed Dunne's original scheme, local residents now appealed against the council's ruling, which, even without the tower, would have allowed a development that would have dwarfed the rest of Victorian Ballsbridge. Their petitions were heard by An Bord Pleanála, the body that decides on appeals against planning decisions made by local authorities. At the hearings, residents argued that Dunne's towers would fundamentally alter the residential character of the area. In its January 2009 ruling, An Bord Pleanála agreed, finding the development 'at odds with the established character of Ballsbridge' and overturning the planning permission that had been granted by the council. By that point, the property market had crashed and the banks had gone bust. Dunne, who had continued to borrow heavily on the understanding that permission would be granted for the site, was in an impossible position.

The battle over Dunne's plans was generally portrayed in the media as an archetypal clash between a brash developer and a conservative local bourgeoisie wishing to preserve what An Bord Pleanála called the 'character' of their sub-urb. The irony is that the battlefield was an ugly commercial triangle that already bore little relationship to the Victorian residential streets surrounding it. Jurys and the Berkeley Court were a pair of ageing seven-storey concrete hulks. Hume House and the Veterinary College, equally unpre-possessing, can have inspired little local affection. I walked south-east along Pembroke Road, passing the western per-imeter of the hotel formerly known as Jurys; it's now known as the Ballsbridge Hotel. (In January 2012, a syndi-cate of Dunne's creditors took control of both hotels.) Iron railings enclose the Ballsbridge Hotel, and behind the railings is a row of mature trees; beyond the trees is a car park that surrounds the hotel. The trees pre-date the hotel buildings: mainly holm oak, they were planted there when the site was occupied by the Trinity College Botanic Gar-den. Across the car park is the main entrance into the hotel, to the left of which is a pub built into a low-slung rectangu-lar concrete bunker that contains a number of function rooms – including the ballroom where, on an annual basis, my parents used to attend a Christmas party held by my father's employers. A burgundy-coloured sign above a separate entrance to the bunker called the single-storey extension a 'Conference Centre'. This had been turned into a supermarket run by Gayle Killilea, named 'D4 Stores', once it became clear that Dunne wasn't going to get anything new built on the site – but D4 Stores didn't last very long.

After standing for a while outside the Ballsbridge

Hotel, I continued south-east along Pembroke Road, reaching at the boundary of the hotel's car park the derelict former veterinary school of University College Dublin and then Hume House, an eight-storey red-brick office building. A large sign outside advertised office space within: several floors were unoccupied.

The veterinary school, meanwhile, stands empty. As I walked by, I noted the relatively basic and functional building: red brick, three storeys. On the porch above the boarded-up front entrance are carvings of animal skulls. The front gate was secured with a padlock and chain. Weeds grew between paving stones inside the gate. A number of signs were fixed to the wooden boards used to secure the windows, warning potential trespassers of the Occupiers' Liability Act 1995 ('The owner of these lands cannot be held responsible for injury, loss or damage to persons or property, however caused. Entry on to this property is entirely at person's own risk'), and giving the contact details of the security firm that oversees the site. From Shelbourne Road, to the east, I was able to glimpse broken windows, through which I could see the kind of shelves used as pigeon-holes to deliver post to staff and students in academic buildings. When I worked in University College Dublin's Belfield campus, I delivered letters and packages to such pigeonholes all the time, and so it seemed odd to see a similar working environment in this context – as a ruin. The building's peculiar desolation was also an isolated reminder of the fate that had been intended for Hume

House and the still-functional hotels: to be abandoned, destroyed, replaced and forgotten.

Further along the road in Ballsbridge is the AIB Bank-centre, the sprawling concrete campus headquarters of Allied Irish Banks, one of the largest banks in Ireland. In April 2006, in the middle of his Ballsbridge spree, Seán Dunne jointly bought the Bankcentre, paying €200 million of the €378 million cost. The property was then leased back to the bank. This sale happened in the same year that Bank of Ireland sold its modernist offices in Baggot Street – AIB, too, must have sensed that the market had peaked, though its lenders must not have got the memo: it required an even bigger bail-out than Bank of Ireland. As I walked towards the building, which stands just across the road from the Royal Dublin Society grounds on Merrion Road, I passed countless bank staff on lunch, their identity cards swinging from the lanyards that hung around their necks.

I walked past the heavily fortified British embassy, a grey postmodernist building that resembled a train shed and was surrounded by heavy granite perimeter walls bearing multiple CCTV cameras, nodding to a policeman who stood flush against the wall. As I turned on to Shrewsbury Road I saw another policeman in the distance, walking on the same side of the road as me – his bright-yellow high-visibility jacket was unmistakable.

I crossed the road, and continued onwards.

The South African embassy has recently relocated to

a huge mansion called Ouragh, which stands at 20A Shrewsbury Road. Granite steps lead up to a black front door, above which, embedded in the red brick, there is a stone arch. There are huge bay windows on either side of the door, and dormer windows protrude from the red-tiled roof. Although its design superficially resembles that of the Victorian houses that line the road, Ouragh is just over ten years old.

The site had been bought by Seán Dunne in 1999; the house was named after an area near his birthplace of Tullow. Having a home on Shrewsbury Road spoke of someone really making it, but there's something telling about the kind of house Dunne ended up with: a product of the Celtic Tiger years that strained to replicate the style of the neighbouring houses. It doesn't quite fit in, however: it is too large, too close to the road.

If you were to pick one image to sum up the era of boom and bust, you may well choose this one, taken by a *New York Times* photographer inside Ouragh in 2009: Seán Dunne stands in the foreground, on the right; Gayle Killilea, on the left and in the background, is sitting. Dunne wears a waistcoat, pink shirt, blue tie and an expression somewhere between a scowl and a smile. Killilea smiles brightly, a considerably younger woman with blonde hair, her head at a slight angle, wearing a tight white blouse. In the background you can see a plush, dark-walled room with a parquet wooden floor on which a large red and gold mat sits, just in front of a white fireplace. The coffee table in the centre has the same parquetry pattern as the floor. On a table on the left of the image, visible just above Killilea's head, sits a chess set with oversized pieces. You can feel the anxiety pulsing through the photo: two people attempting to portray a life of luxury while everything that underpins their wealth and status is unravelling. By the time I walked along Shrewsbury Road, Dunne and Killilea had long moved to America, and in March 2013 Dunne had filed for bankruptcy there, while opposing bankruptcy proceedings in Ireland.

A bit beyond Ouragh, I came to a house named Walford, a red-brick mansion with black-and-white-painted gables, multiple chimneys and many, many windows. There was an A4 sheet bearing an application for planning permission encased behind clear plastic along the house's garden wall. In 2005, a company called Matsack Nominees Ltd had bought Walford for €63.2 million, but it was widely believed that the real buyer was Gayle Killilea. The house had previously belonged to Patrick Duggan, the co-founder of the Irish Glass Bottle Company, whose site at Ringsend was soon to become an extremely expensive waste land. After the sale of Walford, it was reported that Shrewsbury Road was one of the most expensive residential streets in the world. Then the crash happened. In 2013, the house sold for €14 million, less than a quarter of the 2005 price. Walford's perimeter hedge seemed a little overgrown; some weeds grew in its roof guttering and its brickwork looked dilapidated, with grey, vein-like marks trailing down the façade indicating where ivy had been pulled from the wall. The house appeared unoccupied and in need of some restoration, especially when compared to its well-tended neighbours.

From one perspective, Ballsbridge – with its hotels which had somehow avoided the wrecking ball, the office block with a couple of empty floors, the boarded-up shell of the veterinary school, the deserted mansions on desirable streets – was a sort of ghost town, studded with object lessons for a country that had rendered itself an economic disaster zone. But that was not the only available perspective. I looked back along Shrewsbury Road. Parked next to the kerb were a number of vans belonging to workers who were carrying out repairs and refurbishment work on some of the big houses – cleaning granite, replastering, laying new driveways. Signs hung from the iron railings outside the houses, advertising the workmen's ability to revive buildings that were over a hundred years old. Shrewsbury Road, in full summer leaf, looked perfect, ageless, untouched by anything around it. Within a week of my visit, newspapers were reporting that, after a number of years of dramatic decline, the Irish residential property market was beginning to pick up again.

10. Suburban Decay

Continuing southward on Shrewsbury Road, I came to the T-junction with Ailesbury Road, a tree-lined avenue that runs east from Donnybrook to near the sea at Sydney Parade. While the most expensive location on the Dublin edition of the Monopoly board game is Shrewsbury Road, it is closely followed in price by Ailesbury Road. In the real-world residential property market, they are similarly ranked.

I turned left on Ailesbury Road and walked eastward. Pristine red-brick and granite mansions housed the embassies of China, France, Poland. I continued until, just before the junction with Merrion Road, I reached number 2. The name of the house, Coolbawn, was painted in gold letters on a black background on each of its stone gateposts. A 'Sold' sign was posted outside.

The seller was Thomas McFeely.

A month before I walked down Ailesbury Road, I had gone to meet Ursula Graham, the owner of an apartment in Priory Hall, near Clongriffin, on the northern fringe of the city. When I talked to her on the phone to arrange the visit, Ursula had told me that the site was guarded by security men, who were wary of letting people they didn't know into the complex, especially if they were journalists. She said I should bring a backpack and keep my camera hidden in there.

It was a warm evening in the last week of July when I took the number 15 bus through the city centre, along the North Strand, through Fairview and north along the Malahide Road, past industrial estates, small shopping precincts and seemingly unending rows of two-storey suburban housing. The bus reached a crossroads, two corners of which were occupied by buildings – a hotel to the north-west and a fitness centre and supermarket to the south-east. The south-west corner was open, uneven grassland, while the north-east corner was hidden behind hoardings shielding an expanse of land that had been intended for housing. The bus turned east and passed between recent residential developments before turning north at a roundabout beside a derelict church. I got off near a junction, on either side of which stood two grey towers which I recognized from a Priory Hall brochure. Between the grey towers, access to the development was blocked by a light wire fence that ran across the road, in the centre of which was a small Portakabin occupied by security men.

The ground-floor shop unit in each tower was boarded up with plywood: an empty hair salon, a deserted grocery store. Still clinging to the plywood sheets were panels advertising the development. These featured photos evidently intended to evoke mobility: a train, a plane, an M50 motorway sign, a happy young couple jogging. The paint had begun to peel from the walls. The apartments above the shop units were also vacant: a pair of French doors that opened on to the balcony of a third-floor apartment was thrown wide open, as if it were a sunny Sunday morning.

Behind the wire fence that blocked the entrance, I could see a wide road whose central median was over-grown with weeds. On each side of the road, which was empty apart from the presence of a couple of parked cars, were six-storey apartment buildings clad in a com-bination of brown brick and orange panelling; this panelling was imprinted with a woodgrain pattern that can only be seen close up. From a distance, the upper storeys gave the impression of being constructed from orange-and-white-coloured pieces of oversized Lego that had been slotted together slightly haphazardly, an effect I assumed was intentional.

As I stood at the entrance looking around, a blonde woman wearing a white shirt and black-rimmed glasses waved at me from behind the fence, then stepped through a gap to greet me. This was Ursula. She led me through the fence, and we walked with an air of casualness past the security men, who knew her and didn't seem suspicious of me and my backpack. We continued towards the ground-floor entrance to the apartment block to our right. Ursula typed a code into the keypad and pushed the door. There was a rapid beeping; the door would not budge.

She tried the code again, and again. Still the door would not budge. I became aware of the security men approach-ing and suddenly felt nervous; but they were just keen to help us. They tried, failed, then tried once more: the door swung open and Ursula and I climbed the stairs.

A brass number 5 was fixed to the door of Ursula's apartment, and there were two keyholes, one halfway down the door and one near the top. Ursula turned a key in each of the locks and pushed the door: it didn't move. I had heard the lock mechanisms click, and I wondered if perhaps the wood of the door had warped a little, causing it to jam. I pushed at it with the palm of my hand; although there was slight give, it didn't open. I went at it again with my right shoulder, trying to put my body weight into it; my shoulder bounced off the door and it juddered open. Inside, an alarm chirped every couple of minutes while we walked from room to room. The combined kitchen and dining room, the largest room in the apartment, was almost completely empty, except for a white internal door, unscrewed from the kitchen's door frame and propped up against the silver-flock-wallpapered wall.

We gazed out the window, towards the block of flats opposite. Ursula pointed to the duplex apartments teetering on the roof and told me that they didn't have a viable fire exit: one of a number of fire-code violations that had brought about the evacuation of Priory Hall, nearly two years earlier. You could see staining on the concrete walls. All the windows were dully discoloured with two years of dust. We walked out to the balcony, and Ursula showed me where rainwater would cascade down from the terrace of the apartment above.

Owing to a court order, residents couldn't return to live in the apartment block until it was made safe. No one knew when that would be.

I asked Ursula what she wanted to happen to Priory Hall.

'I think it needs to be knocked to the ground,' she said.

Thomas McFeely, the developer of Priory Hall, is a portly, grey-haired, moustachioed man in his mid-sixties. His life has been one of almost psychedelic extremes, and yet it is also a representative life: much of recent Irish history is embodied, magnified and distorted in his various incarnations. 'I fought for a socialist republic and I still believe in it,' he told an interviewer in 2012, as his multimillion-euro empire collapsed around him.

McFeely, who grew up on a farm in County Derry, was a twenty-year-old bricklayer living in London when police attacked civil rights marchers in Derry on 5 October 1968. He told the journalist Susan McKay, author of a probing 2012 profile in the *Guardian*, that 'the 5th of October brought me back'. By the late 1970s, he had been in and out of prison a couple of times, having blown up a dole office in Antrim and carried out an armed robbery on a post office. After the robbery, he holed up in a rural house that was put under siege by security forces. 'It was a bit Wild West,' he said of the siege, in which he shot a policeman (who survived). In 1977, McFeely was sentenced to twenty-six years in prison, which he began to serve in one of the recently built H-Block units at HMP Maze, which were constructed in reinforced concrete and intended to withstand bomb blasts.

When Britain ceased to recognize IRA members as political prisoners, McFeely, as the IRA officer in command of H-Block 5, led those who refused to wear the prison uniform. The strike escalated into a dirty protest, in which prisoners urinated in their cells and smeared excrement on the walls. McFeely was subsequently chosen by the IRA leadership as a hunger striker. The strike was called off when one prisoner, Seán McKenna, was on the brink of death. McFeely, by now temporarily blind as a result of malnutrition, was opposed to calling it off. 'I was fully prepared to die,' he later said.

McFeely was released from prison in 1989 and moved to Dublin to work as a bricklayer on building sites. Within a couple of years, he had amassed enough money to buy a pub in Dungiven, County Derry. He was involved in some small property developments in Donegal and Dublin. Then in 1998 he joined with Larry O'Mahony, a resident of Shrewsbury Road, to build the Plaza Hotel in Tallaght, for an estimated €40 million.

McFeely's evolution from bomber and gunman to high-stakes property developer made him an object of media curiosity, and he used to entertain journalists by pointing to the collected works of Lenin on the bookshelves of Coolbawn, or by quoting Marx's observation that 'religion is the opium of the people' when discussing his own rejection of Catholicism. He had been a member of the League of Communist Republicans, a splinter group based in the Maze. Their programme demanded from the state 'a home suitable to the citizen's needs', a modest request for something which McFeely, once he got into the housing business himself, found it strangely difficult to provide.

Ursula Graham was thirty years old when she moved in to Priory Hall. It was 2007, and a lot of people were buying unbuilt houses and apartments from developers on the basis of drawings and brochures. By that time, the steep rise in Irish property prices had become self-reinforcing: there was a widespread feeling that if you didn't buy *now*, you might lose your last chance to get on the 'property ladder'. Priory Hall wasn't far from Coolock, where Ursula had grown up and where members of her family still lived, and she was happy with the apartment on offer: two bedrooms, a kitchen–dining room and a balcony. A glossy brochure promised buyers an 'urban village' between the city and the country, and drew attention to some local ruins that provided 'a pleasant link to the past'. But Priory Hall was wholly about the future – you were buying something that didn't exist yet, that would be different, better. The brochure made liberal use of quotation marks: when it said that the development would offer 'an instantly "authentic" connection with the street', or when it described Priory Hall as a 'nicely "contained" development', it was not clear who, if anyone, was being quoted. Perhaps inevitably, it appealed to the potential buyer in the tried and tested language of the garden-city estate, calling the apartment project 'your dream of a contemporary-style home ... midway between the trimmings of the city and the trappings of the country'.

Ursula looked at the plans, then signed up and bought her apartment for €275,000, taking a mortgage for the full amount. The apartments were soon built, and Ursula moved in. In the beginning, everything seemed perfect, just like the scale model reproduced in the brochure. But it wasn't long before things started to go wrong. During heavy rainfall, water seeped into the apartments. Windows and balcony doors seemed badly sealed, allowing water in even after they had been patched up by workmen. Ursula's upstairs neighbours had to lift their floorboards four times as a result of flooding in 2009. Ursula showed me where a paving stone at the corner of one apartment block had been lifted by a resident investigating the flooding; the stone had hidden the fact that the drainpipe leading down the side of the building didn't connect to a hole bored in the concrete below.

In the scheme of things at Priory Hall, the drainage problems were relatively trivial. In November 2008, a fire broke out in one of the apartments. An alarm was triggered, and when firefighters arrived they checked the fire panel, which was meant to indicate which apartment was affected. The firemen arrived at the door of the apartment, only to find that it was the wrong one. Eventually they located the fire in a completely different apartment.

Under legislation introduced in the 1990s, developers were allowed to 'self-certify' the safety status of their developments. Plans would be drawn up and submitted to the planning authority, which would then grant permission. The contractors and subcontractors who carried out the work would attest that it had been done according to the regulations laid down by the planning authority. The developer's architect would then inspect the certificates and the building, and issue a certificate of compliance if they thought the work had been done correctly. Dublin City Council was entitled to undertake inspections but, in practice, only a small percentage of newly built properties were inspected.

The November 2008 fire in Priory Hall alerted the fire services to the fault with the fire panel, but it wasn't until September 2009 that the council served notices ordering a fire-safety management system be put in place and the inspection and maintenance of emergency lighting, fire-detection and alarm systems and fire-door assemblies. A programme of works to address these issues was agreed. When the council inspected the buildings in November of that year, not all the remedial work had been done, so, shortly before Christmas, the council moved its own tenants – who occupied 23 of the 187 apartments – out of the buildings. The council also informed the private owners that the development was potentially dangerous, and the council's chief fire officer ordered that the underground car parks be shut, owing to the flooding issue.

Further deadlines imposed by the council were missed by McFeely's company. In May 2011, the council's housing department had commissioned consultants to inspect some of the council's own units at Priory Hall and to write a report on their findings. When Donal Casey, a council fire officer, testified at the High Court on 14 October 2011, he said that although earlier fire inspections had been carried out – he himself had examined Priory Hall in July 2009 and said he was 'pretty much horrified' by what he saw – they had been of common areas of the complex. It wasn't until later in 2011 that the Fire Brigade had surveyed an apartment in Priory Hall. Casey told the High Court that he was shocked when he saw the consultants' report. He carried out two inspections of apartments (on 12 and 21 September) and immediately informed the chief fire officer of the situation: because of structural defects, if a fire that started in an apartment got into the external cavity wall, it could extend to the entire building, as there was no barrier in place to stop it spreading. In court, Casey said that what was built in Priory Hall was 'very different' from what had been stipulated on fire-safety certificates that were issued for the development. In early October 2011, Dublin City Council wrote to residents of Priory Hall, informing them of the potential of serious risk in the case of a fire and that the council's fire officer would be seeking an evacuation order in court. (The letter also cited problems with the gas and electricity installations in individual apartments, in addition to the issues with the fire-alarm system.) An evacuation order was granted by the High Court. Residents were given a week to leave their homes.

This wasn't the first time a McFeely development had been found to be seriously defective. In 2006, residents of Na Cluainte, an 84-house development in Portarlington, County Offaly, claimed the estate was in an 'appalling state' two years after the last house had been built there. A sizeable portion of one resident's back garden was permanently under water, and there were problems with dangerous fencing and unfinished road surfaces. Offaly County Council initiated High Court proceedings against McFeely, calling for remedial work to be carried out. Ard Dealgan, a five-storey apartment building built by McFeely in Dundalk, was served with a closure notice by Dundalk Town Council on 6 October 2009, after an inspection revealed the building did not meet the standards stipulated in the fire-safety certificate issued by the council. Its twenty-eight tenants were told that they would have to move out, leaving the building empty. Subsequently, the *Dundalk Democrat* reported numerous fires at the empty property, which was being used by homeless people. By early 2014, its ground-floor doors and windows had been bricked up. McFeely had also built Áras na Cluaine, a development of 198 apartments in Clondalkin; in February 2011, Dublin City Council asked the High Court for an order to prevent occupation of the building, as the fire officer believed there was a high risk to occupants as a result of poor fire-safety provision.

'Everything was done in a rush,' McFeely told Susan

McKay. 'The attitude was get it up, get it off, get on to the next job. Come back and finish it later.'

Priory Hall is part of a troubled belt of development known as the North Fringe, a higher-density strip of residential housing, shops and hotels that runs along the city side of the boundary line between Dublin city and Fingal. In 1999, Dublin Corporation (the precursor to Dublin City Council) re-zoned for residential use a vast area of largely agricultural land between the Malahide Road and the north–south railway line. The plan emphasized a need for a 'coherent urban structure' based on the guidelines laid down in the Corporation's Dublin City Development Plan, which adopted 'an urban model which places public transport, increased densities and a mix of uses at its core'.

Developers who had speculated on the re-zoning by buying up fields in north Dublin quickly made big money. In 2000, a Bovale sold 152 acres of the newly re-zoned land at Balgriffin for around £45 million (€57 million); Bovale had bought the land in the mid-1980s. Developer John Mulryan bought five hundred acres of land on the former Baldoyle Racecourse for £30 million in the mid-1990s, then, after it had been re-zoned for housing, sold a 50 per cent stake for €95 million in 2004. Other landowners, such as Gannon Homes and Shannon Homes, had also built up reserves of land in the area with the intention of large-scale development.

In 2004, work began on eight hundred housing units at Beau Park, part of the new town of Clongriffin, built by Menolly Homes and Killoe Developments on a site purchased from developer Gerry Gannon, who had built up his land holdings in the area over the years. 'We expect to sell three hundred homes by Christmas off plans, and, when we start, we are going to keep on selling,' a spokesperson for Menolly said. The first phase of Beau Park was a low-rise housing estate, but it was soon joined by medium-rise apartments. By 2006 the first residents were moving into Beau Park, and by March 2008 the town centre at Clongriffin was complete: apartment blocks with commercial premises at ground level, an underground car park and a building intended to house a supermarket. Also promised were a sixty-bedroom hotel, a multiscreen cinema and a railway station. As early as 2006, adverts for the Beau Park development used the station as a means of attracting buyers: 'Want to be at the centre of everything? We have just the ticket.'

Sales of apartments slowed down, and, by the time the station eventually opened, on 19 April 2010, the mood in Clongriffin was considerably different. It was expected that €1 billion of loans to Gannon would be taken into NAMA (the National Asset Management Agency – the 'bad bank' formed by the Irish government in late 2009 to acquire property loans from banks in return for government bonds), while Menolly Homes was also badly affected by poor investments. Journalists visiting Clongriffin to report on the station's opening found unfinished housing developments and a large number of empty shop units.

I first visited Clongriffin in 2008, after a friend of mine had bought an apartment on its main street. My bus passed huge advertising hoardings that lined the roads around Belmayne, a development at the western end of the North Fringe. The images created for the Belmayne campaign had become notorious. The most famous of these featured a woman draped across a kitchen island while a man leaned vampirishly over her, offering a platter of strawberries. In the background, you could see two bottles of champagne sitting near the sink and, through the sliding door, a hint of banal suburban normality: wooden fencing and the rear windows of neighbouring houses. The slogan was 'Gorgeous living comes to Dublin'.

Belmayne was marketed like a perfume: at its 2007 launch, minor celebrities turned out to walk the red carpet towards the development's futuristic marketing suite. Two-bedroom homes started at €315,000. In 2012, Dublin Fire Brigade's chief fire officer found that 232 apartments at Belmayne had safety issues that could allow a fire to spread, and ordered the developer to carry out repairs. (By July 2013, work had been completed in all but seventeen developments, with work due to begin on eight, while residents were refusing access to the remaining nine.)

Priory Hall never had the glitz of Belmayne, nor the ambition of Clongriffin, and it is a relatively small development. But in an area that has become synonymous with the follies of the boom, it is the most notorious of all.

*

A few days before I met Ursula at Priory Hall, Fiachra Daly, a 38-year-old Priory Hall resident, was found dead in the temporary accommodation he shared with his partner and children; he had committed suicide. Daly had been extremely active in publicizing the plight of Priory Hall residents, giving interviews to the press and allowing himself to be photographed while moving out of the apartment in October 2011 – one published picture showed him dismantling the cot of his six-month-old baby. A month after his death, his widow, Stephanie Meehan, publicly shared an email she had sent to the Taoiseach, Enda Kenny. She wrote that, a week before Fiachra's death, they had received demands from banks 'looking for payment of arrears on a property that we can't live in'.

In the months after being evacuated from the development, the Priory Hall residents had worked out temporary solutions with their mortgage providers, but these arrangements were far from ideal. Ursula told me that she had a moratorium in place on her mortgage: it was agreed with her lender that she wouldn't make payments while she couldn't live in the apartment. But interest continued to accrue on the loan outstanding, and she calculated that, by October 2013, she was approximately €20,000 in arrears on her mortgage. She said that residents feared they would be forced into bankruptcy by this situation unless a solution could be arrived at.

*

In 2009, when a journalist visited Thomas McFeely at his home on Ailesbury Road, the developer brandished a Celtic cross engraved with the faces of his fellow hunger strikers for the photographer. He spoke of his first night in Dublin, when he slept in a car and had only £240 to his name. Twenty years later, he was a multimillionaire developer. The journalist asked him how this transformation had happened. 'There has been no transformation,' McFeely replied. 'I've just brought the energy and determination I gave to the IRA to the world of business.' He said that he had more respect for street-sweepers or barmen than fellow property developers, who he described as 'arrogant, egotistical and anaemic'. His Bentley, his mansion – all the trappings of wealth valued by his wealthy neighbours – were appropriated by McFeely, then presented as two-fingers to the establishment. He kept the Celtic cross in his front window, visible to passers-by.

When Dublin City Council sought the evacuation order for Priory Hall, in mid-October 2011, it assumed that progress would be made on the requisite repairs in a matter of weeks. McFeely's company, Coalport, was given until 28 November to complete the work. Priory Hall residents were initially housed in nearby hotels, then relocated to empty properties in adjoining estates, the cost being borne grudgingly by the council.

After a week, the council's fire-safety officer was broadly satisfied with how the work was progressing, but expressed concern about the external structure of the buildings. A few days later, the developers and workers were ordered to leave the site because of a lack of progress. McFeely said he didn't have the funds to finish the repairs.

Bankruptcy proceedings were initiated in December 2011 against McFeely, and hearings scheduled for the following month. But in mid-January 2012 McFeely filed for bankruptcy in the British courts, as a number of other troubled Irish developers have done. His reason for this was the differing implications of bankruptcy in Ireland and the UK: bankruptcy terms in Ireland last twelve years, whereas, in the UK, they are typically twelve months, allowing the bankrupt person to write off debts and resume business relatively quickly. (The term of Irish bankruptcy was reduced to three years as a result of legislation introduced in December 2013.) The irony of McFeely, unrepentant Irish republican, attempting to use his UK citizenship as a shield from his debts and responsibilities in Ireland didn't go unnoticed by the media.

The key challenge to McFeely's attempts to secure bankruptcy in the UK came from Theresa McGuinness, who had bought a house in Rush, County Dublin, from the developer in 2006. The house had serious structural problems, and McGuinness was awarded €100,000 in damages, a sum that McFeely failed to pay. McGuinness had initiated Irish bankruptcy proceedings against him in December 2011; she challenged his UK application and, in July 2012, succeeded. Later that month, McFeely was declared bankrupt in Ireland.

Throughout this process, McFeely had held on to the house in Ailesbury Road, for which he had taken out a €9.5 million mortgage in 2005. Once he was declared bankrupt, moves were quickly made to repossess the property. The High Court gave McFeely and his family until 10 August 2012 to vacate the house; the sheriff repossessed it on behalf of NAMA that evening. It emerged that McFeely hadn't made a mortgage payment in three years.

On Friday, 19 September 2013, tradesmen working in Coolbawn found in its bathroom €140,000 in cash, made up of bundles of €50 notes. The tradesmen alerted their employer, who contacted the gardaí. A thorough search of the property located another €60,000 in cash, also in €50 notes. The official assignee for McFeely's bankruptcy requested that a reward of €10,000 be split between the new owners of Coolbawn and the tradesmen who had located the cash. The couple who now owned the house asked that their share be given to Stephanie Meehan, the partner of the deceased Fiachra Daly. McFeely denied the cash was his and claimed it had been planted by gardaí.

Ursula had warned me that there might be rats. They could sometimes be seen running around in the car park. We walked down the stairs, past the lift that stood with its doors open at basement level, its floor rusted a burnt orange from the water that had flowed down the shaft over the years. She told me that the button to call the lift had been soaked in water, and residents worried about being electrocuted. The stale smell of standing water was overpowering.

The car park was dark and empty. Ursula said that a friend of hers had parked a car there one rainy night and come back to find it floating away. She pointed up to the metal grilles above – these provided air and light, but also let rainwater into the car park. I looked around: there were no gratings in the tarmac to allow water to drain away.

We made our way out of the rear entrance to Ursula's apartment block, avoiding the attention of security guards. Next to the door was a terrace belonging to one of the ground-floor apartments, with potted plants, long forgotten and dead from lack of care, their grey branches skeletal against the orange plastic panels of the external wall. In the next terrace, a child's mountain bike lay twisted on the grey paving stones, its chain rusted and its front wheel missing.

Once the evacuation order from the council came, people moved out quickly. They took what they thought essential and left what they didn't want. Along a wall on the opposite side of the development, black plastic refuse sacks lay scattered alongside the base of a single bed. Elsewhere, I saw a pile of discoloured clothes that looked like they had been left out to dry next to an upturned baby rocker, the grey material of which had begun to turn green with moss. I stumbled across strange juxtapositions: a broken wooden chair next to a car's spare tyre, both discarded on the paving stones outside an exit door.

It was difficult to know whether the residents of Priory Hall would ever get the resolution they wanted. In the meantime, the rotting hulk of the development stood to remind them of the economic and psychological pain caused by Thomas McFeely's rebirth as a developer, and the inadequate regulations that had enabled him, for many years, to thrive. In every deserted apartment in Priory Hall, there was once life; now, there was nothing except dampness, silence and an ever-accelerating decay.

We walked down the road between the apartment blocks. Nothing stirred to break the silence. Nothing moved. I hadn't seen any rats.

'It's spooky, isn't it?' Ursula said.

We looked up towards an apartment on the second floor. In the window were plastic decorations stuck to the glass: skulls and ghosts. Ursula said that the apartment's residents and their children had moved out just before Hallowe'en – as had everyone else at Priory Hall. No one had returned to remove the decorations.

11. Flight Path

Setting out from my friend Jonathan's apartment in Clongriffin, we were heading north – but a vast unbuilt waste land, surrounded by tall black wooden hoardings, was in the way. So we skirted the hoardings until we got to the far side of the waste land, then turned eastward along the row of hulking apartment blocks at Marrsfield – red-brick walls, metal balconies, wooden panelling. Passing a single-storey modernist building that had been used as a showroom for the apartments, we climbed through a gap in a low fence and followed the course of the River Mayne eastward. The railway line was elevated here, and the river ran through one of two red-brick arches; we went through the other arch, which involved climbing over a pile of rubbish. Beyond the railway line, we crossed the river via a makeshift bridge consisting of three metal poles, a wooden plank and a wire fence underneath that acted as a kind of safety net. In the distance to the south, across the waste ground and beyond a water-filled hollow, Clongriffin looked like a city on an alien planet: self-contained, surrounded by hostile territory.

We clambered on to a recently built concrete bridge, impeccably clad in stone, stranded in untidy terrain to the east of the railway line; Jonathan suggested that this was a folly improvised by bored builders. To one side of the bridge lay a builder's white plastic safety helmet and assorted building-site bric-a-brac: plastic piping, a block of wood, a torn plastic refuse bag. Not far away, pristine tarmac covered entire streets that ran amongst the scrubland, empty of buildings. Rectangles of red asphalt marked parking spaces for lines of houses yet to be built.

If the land on which we stood showed clues of an unrealized future, it also had a history you couldn't immediately discern. Starting in the mid-nineteenth century, this was the site of Baldoyle Racecourse. Racing was suspended between 1861 and 1865, owing to crowd trouble; when the racecourse reopened, it had been upgraded significantly and alcohol was no longer on sale in the marquees. The grounds were enclosed and privately policed in order to root out violent activity. Prior to their enclosure, they had played host to 'illegal side-shows, roulette tables, thimble men and cardsharps', according to Michael J. Hurley's history of the area. In 1874, a journalist praised 'the commodious and comfortable stands, the facilities for seeing the course – a model in its way – the number and quality of the horses starting in the different races, the natural advantages of the situation, where a pleasant landscape is on one side, and a picturesque view of the sea on the other'. Violence returned to the racecourse in 1940, when a feud between bookmakers led to two stabbings. After years of decline, the last race was held in Baldoyle in August 1972.

A bit over a year later, on the afternoon of 31

October 1973, a helicopter landed on the old racecourse.
Three men were bundled from the Alouette into a waiting
car, which sped away. The hijacked helicopter had come
from the exercise yard of Dublin's Mountjoy Prison,
where it had collected three IRA prisoners, including
Chief of Staff Séamus Twomey, before flying away again.
The Wolfe Tones quickly recorded a ballad celebrating
the episode, 'The Helicopter Song', which was banned
by the Irish government; nevertheless, it remained at
number one in the Irish charts for four weeks, until it
was ousted by Slade's 'Merry Xmas, Everybody'.

The River Mayne spread out into a wetland, which we
negotiated carefully, eventually reaching the Coast Road
and the Portmarnock estuary. This was our true starting
point: the plan was to walk to Dublin airport, a few kilometres to the west, tracking the flight path as closely as
we could. Every couple of minutes a low-flying plane
descended directly over our heads, hurtling westward.
We turned from the road and followed the planes. Soon,
we reached a thorny hedgerow and, not wanting to divert
unless absolutely necessary, climbed through, emerging
in a ploughed field. We were unprepared for the sound
of gunfire.

We ducked to the ground. The crumbled earth looked
as though it had been neatly combed.

'Those were shots,' Jonathan said.

There was nowhere to go that would be any safer than
where we were. We crouched low near the hedgerow
and waited.

This was private property. We were trespassing. We knew that. But we hadn't expected to be peppered with buckshot. Our journey had only just begun; was it to end here?

Shots rang out again. And again.

The longer we stayed there, the clearer it became that the shots were coming at regular intervals – too regular, it seemed to me, for a human to be pulling the trigger. I decided that what we were hearing was a bird-scaring device, but Jonathan wasn't convinced.

We could see a gap in a perimeter hedge to our left. To get there, we would have to cross the field. We stayed close to the ground and picked our way carefully to safety. Soon we had reached the Moyne Road, which took us west, past a site of incomplete semi-detached houses, and on to the Malahide Road, which brought us north.

The ancient stone roof of St Doulagh's Church seemed vulnerable, with a passenger jet roaring over its roof every minute or so. On this day, the planes were wobbling in the crosswinds.

Once, in 2006, slumped in a window seat on the right-hand side of an aircraft that must have been passing directly over St Doulagh's, I looked out of the window towards a large house to the north: Abbeville. I pictured the old man inside, ill now – confined to his bed, even – pottering around at the end of his days. Except that Charles Haughey was already dead, and I had momentarily forgotten his absence.

Not far beyond the church, we reached a petrol station, and Jonathan went in to buy coffee and Danish pastries. We sat in the garage forecourt, resting on a low plastic seat in the form of a black and white cow intended for children.

It was said that, if you threw a pin into the pond next to St Doulagh's and then bathed your eyes in the water, any soreness would be cured. It struck me that the same kind of belief which encouraged people to throw pins into ponds and to build churches such as St Doulagh's also sustained their faith in other things: political parties, the property market. The Irish property boom was underpinned by the conviction that prices would increase for ever. When entrenched beliefs are overturned, people will believe in nothing, or anything.

When we'd heard a sequence of loud bangs in a field, we thought it was gunfire. Even now, we still weren't sure.

The suburbs of Dublin are dotted with the physical remnants of old beliefs. Any number of castles, churches and holy wells were destroyed to make way for housing, but many survive. Around three kilometres south from the garage where we sat drinking coffee, next to a roundabout just before you reach Clongriffin, you can see the remains of an old church, Grange Abbey. In the oratory there is a gap in the wall, which was said to cure headache or toothache when you placed your head in it. The road that leads to the church, linking Clongriffin with the rest of the city, is called Hole in the Wall Road. A few hundred metres away from Grange Abbey, Donaghmede's modern church stands on the edge of a piece of land purchased by Charles Haughey in 1959. This was the site of Grangemore, a large Georgian house on 45 acres. At the suggestion of the property developer Matt Gallagher, Haughey had bought the house, for £13,000, with a view to getting the land re-zoned for housing. The lands were indeed soon re-zoned. In 1969, Haughey, who was Minister for Finance at the time, sold Grangemore to the Gallaghers for £260,000 and bought Abbeville, a grand Georgian estate at Kinsealy. Accusations were made by the opposition that Haughey had benefited from provisions he had himself inserted into the 1968 Finance Act, allowing him to avoid tax on the sale. Although the Grangemore deal didn't wholly account for the fortune he subsequently accrued, it epitomized the intertwined webs of politics and property development that would shape Dublin's suburban form, and Ireland's economy, in subsequent years. The Gallaghers knocked down Grangemore and built houses on the site.

A few years before Haughey died, he sold Abbeville for development as a golf course and hotel, with the stipulation that he could live out his days there.

Not far from the petrol station, we turned left and headed west along Baskin Lane, passing large bungalows and small farms, until we reached Clonshaugh Road, which we followed across the M1 motorway. From the bridge above the motorway, we could see the giant hangars at Dublin airport sitting on a plateau to the west. To the

east, the highest visible point was a pockmarked emi-
nence: Feltrim Hill. Writing in 1909, Dillon Cosgrave,
a Carmelite priest and local historian, explained that
Feltrim means 'ridge of wolves' and drew attention to
the remains of a windmill at the crest of the slope. Now
it looked much reduced – the ruins of a hill, heavily
quarried.

Dublin airport's site now seems a natural choice: on
largely flat terrain, far from mountain winds and above
sea level. Initially, however, Ireland's civil aircraft operated from Baldonnel in west Dublin. The first Aer Lingus
passenger flight took off from there in 1936. By that
time, the present site of the airport, at Collinstown, had
been chosen for the development of a much larger terminal. Work began at the site in 1937, and by January
1940 the Aer Lingus Dublin–Liverpool service had moved
to the new airport. The art deco terminal building,
designed by Desmond FitzGerald, was suggestive of a
cosmopolitan glamour that was at odds with the protec-
tionist policies being pursued by the government of the
time. The airport was an emblem of Ireland's future –
or, perhaps, a wager on Ireland's future. It was a way of
negotiating the country's place in the world. However,
the airport also became a theatre in which the more
troubling aspects of Irish identity would be rehearsed.

Years before I actually set foot on a plane, my family
and I used to make trips to the airport simply to watch
the planes take off. There were viewing places tucked
away at odd corners of the departure area where you

could watch aircraft taxiing across the apron then pointing their noses towards the sky. Forty years after it had
opened, the airport still had the capacity for romance,
though, at that time, in the 1980s, we watched the planes
from the brutalist Terminal 1 building, with its brown
and orange signs. When you walked through the main
entrance, your bag was scanned by a security man who
stood at an ordinary table with a hand-held scanner.

Security was tight because of a fear of bombs. On
29 November 1975, the day my brother was born, a man
had been killed in an explosion in a men's toilet at the
airport. It was four hours before the body of John
Hayes, who worked at the airport, was recovered; the
delay was due, it was said, to the possibility of there
being further explosive devices among the debris. In
the immediate aftermath of the detonation, a security
officer investigated another bathroom. He found a
toilet-tissue box resting on top of a newspaper; two yellow wires poked out of it. He left the bathroom, to alert
the security team. At 1.40 p.m., that device exploded,
too. The loyalist Ulster Defence Association claimed
responsibility for the bombs, saying the attacks were
carried out as revenge on Dublin and the Irish government for allegedly harbouring members of the IRA. At
the inquest into John Hayes's death, while medical evidence was being given, his widow asked for permission
to leave the room.

Over the years, further threats were made against
the airport. As a result of the 1975 bombing, roof parking

on top of Terminal 1 was discontinued. The coiling concrete ramp leading up to the roof stood as a kind of folly, representing what now seemed an innocent time. Whenever we went to the airport, my dad would point out the car-park structure and explain why it was no longer used.

Jonathan and I made our way through the bushes along an overgrown, disused road past the boarded-up former airport crèche. We were trying to intersect with a public road that led into the airport from the north, past the hangars that were visible from all around. Our journey was nearly at an end.

Jonathan's brother was leaving from the airport for a holiday that afternoon. Jonathan had texted him, but we were too late – he was already on the other side of security, that border between the everyday and the other world of air travel, a demarcation that had intrigued me since I was a child, when at the end of every Christmas holiday we used to wave off my uncle Séamus, who had emigrated to America in the 1980s. During that decade, the airport had become the symbolic space of Irish emigration. Now, emigration scenes had become common again: the terms 'departure' and 'arrival' were more emotionally charged than they had been at any time in the previous twenty years. The fluid international mobility that had become an accepted part of Irish identity in the preceding decade was beginning to harden, to seize up; this time, it seemed, once you went, you were less likely to come back.

The airport's new Terminal 2 building opened in late 2010. Frank McDonald of the *Irish Times* pointed out that, although the 'sweeping curves of the new terminal suggest a swaggering symbol of boom-time Ireland', internally the building exhibits a more positive, orderly image of the country. 'Except for the views out towards Howth and Ballymun, and, indeed, a glimpse of the unloved Terminal 1, it is like being in another country.' In McDonald's survey of the terminal's architectural form, one could detect a tension, characteristic of his work, between a near-utopian faith in the sophisticated ways of other countries and the grubby actuality of life in the Republic of Ireland – the latter exemplified by the 'dilapidated and often chaotic' Terminal 1. Terminal 2 promised an escape from the realities of Irish life – if only Howth and Ballymun could be redacted from the vista. For me, the symbolic nature of the airport wasn't fixed in this way. Shortly after the new terminal opened, I made a number of trips between Dublin and Paris. Although I came to appreciate the new building's architecture, the terminal itself didn't provide escape. Being away did that. And, once I was elsewhere, I came to appreciate that Terminal 2 and the surrounding landscape weren't mutually exclusive, and that both had tales to tell about the evolution of modern Ireland.

It wasn't until after we had walked beyond the big hangars, past the petrol station and across the airport's feeder road, through the hotel car parks between temporary-looking prefabricated buildings still used as offices; it wasn't until we were exhausted and nearly there, nearly at our destination, and we could no longer talk much because we'd burned up so much energy jumping through hedges and over gates and ducking gunfire that may or may not have been gunfire; it wasn't until then, when we had traversed the unused, tarmacked space delineated with white-and-yellow-painted lines and had turned our sights away from the modernist concrete church and the white multi-storey car parks, that I looked up and saw the undulating form of Terminal 2 lurch towards us, as if to welcome our arrival.

12. On Reaching the Liffey

A friend was to accompany me on my trip along the river, but he didn't turn up at our meeting place in the city centre and, when I called him, his mobile phone was turned off. So I pushed on alone. It was about eight o'clock on a Friday morning, and it would soon be low tide.

I stepped off the tram at Heuston station, which is where Dublin's Liffey quays begin. (Upstream from the station, the Liffey is less accessible: public byways are a distance from the river and are often separated from its leafy banks by private land or buildings.) For the past six months I'd been living in the north of England, where my girlfriend had got a job, and on my return, in early March, the weather was pleasant and the city was beginning to vibrate with expectation. I was surprised by the sensation I experienced on coming home to Dublin: I felt relaxed; I enjoyed the atmosphere. I felt, to some degree, like a tourist in an unfamiliar city.

Although the Liffey flows through the very centre of Dublin, and in spite of it being in constant view when you walk the quays or cross a bridge, it nonetheless feels at a peculiar physical remove from the city. It tends to sit low in its bed, and most Dubliners never have reason to navigate it in a boat, let alone swim in it. Its presence is almost wholly visual. It creates a sinuous cleft in the centre of the city, and presents various overfamiliar tableaux: when I cross O'Connell Bridge and glance upstream towards the Four Courts, I see a vista I've viewed perhaps a thousand times before in the flesh, and which is a staple of the iconography of the city. It's only when something reminds you of the river's watery realness – a quay floods, or someone falls into its muddy depths – that this illusion of remoteness is disturbed.

Perhaps it was owing to this illusion that, even while undertaking the explorations I've written about in this book, I never considered getting nearer to the Liffey. And when I eventually started thinking about the possibility of doing so, my curiosity was tinged with apprehension.

Although no longer a conduit for raw sewage, the Liffey on its final approach to Dublin Bay is a murky, tidal, polluted river. My reluctance to explore it had a more fundamental basis, though: I'm scared of water and I was terrified of falling in. It's a fear that has gripped me since, as a child at primary school, I jumped into a pool, landed in the water awkwardly and panicked. I was quickly fished out by lifeguards, but the psychological damage was done: I never climbed into water again and was rarely comfortable near rivers or lakes. Sometimes, the limits of one's world are defined by old fears that may never be shaken. Years after I had established that I was afraid of water, my uncle Lian drowned in the Atlantic off the coast of Galway; it was weeks before his body was retrieved from the surf. One of the reasons I had thought it would be good to have a companion on this walk was that, if I did make it down to the river, my friend could throw me a lifebuoy, or at least raise the alarm if I fell in.

Leaving Heuston station, I dodged my way through the hurrying crowd of commuters and walked in the direction of the Liffey. Upstream, the river curved away to the right. On the south bank, walled with granite down to the water level, the River Camac flowed into the Liffey through an arched outlet in the quay wall from its culvert beneath the station. Resting against the southern abutment was the mutilated torso of a tree from which four branches, each sawn short to differing lengths, stretched arm-like from its trunk, the bark stripped smooth by months or years of battering by the current.

I had made a simple rule for my journey: travelling downstream from Heuston station, I would cross the river at each bridge I reached. Between the station and the mouth of the river, there were seventeen bridges. (An eighteenth, the Rosie Hackett Bridge, between O'Connell Bridge and Butt Bridge, was still under construction when I made my journey.) One of the seventeen – the Loop Line Bridge, which carries mainline trains across the river – is inaccessible by foot, but I resolved to cross the other sixteen.

Thus I commenced with the bridge immediately adjacent to the station, which was originally named to commemorate the visit of King George IV to Dublin in 1821 – lending the area, and the station, the name Kingsbridge. The bridge itself opened to traffic in 1829, and now, renamed Seán Heuston Bridge, it carries Luas trams. Its iron arches were manufactured in the Phoenix Iron Works, which were housed in the stone industrial buildings on the north side of the river.

I was crossing the river again almost immediately, via Frank Sherwin Bridge, a modern road bridge named for a Dublin politician who entertained dubious views on female recruits to the gardaí ('They should not be too good-looking'). Along the south quay wall, between Heuston Bridge and Sherwin Bridge, was a large muddy flat, across which the morning sunlight stretched. Embedded in the river's gloopy sediment were the wheels of upturned bikes, car tyres and hubcaps, lengths of pipe, traffic cones and a perfect-looking gent's umbrella with a wooden handle. Ducks and seagulls picked happily through the thick slop.

In March 2002, near this point on the river, a young woman on a moped hit a pavement on the south quays. She had been on a driving lesson, and so had been accompanied by an instructor on a motorbike. The woman was thrown from the bike over the quay wall into the river. Her fall was cushioned by the soft mudbank on to which she tumbled, and she survived. When the tide is low, such muddy shores can be seen most of the way along the quay walls. For a long time Dubliners associated the mudbanks with the Liffey's noxious smell. In 1864,

Dublin Corporation, responding to demands to clean the river, stated that 'owing to the nature of the foreshore it is quite impossible to remove all the slimy filth that accumulates there'. Four years later the corporation applied disinfectant to the river – but problems with smell and mud continued into the twentieth century. In 1969, the *Irish Times* published a series of three articles entitled 'What Makes the Liffey Filthy?' The accompanying photos showed wide banks of mud – certainly wider than I've ever seen – along either side of the river at low tide. The journalist considered whether rotting vegetation in the mud was responsible for the stink, before deciding that the much smaller but heavily polluted Camac was corrupting the Liffey. The odour is much reduced these days – normally, the river has no noticeable smell, perhaps owing to improved sewage infrastructure – and my own view of the mudbanks was benign: even if they were slimy and possibly smelled bad, they had saved at least one person's life.

The Liffey rises at 550 metres above sea level in an area of boggy ground beside Military Road, not far from Sally Gap in the Wicklow Mountains. At that point, it seems little more than a grassy ditch; I've crossed the Liffey there many times without realizing it. The stream flows under the road, then along the flank of Kippure Mountain in a westerly direction – that is, away from Dublin. Although the distance from its source to its mouth at Dublin Bay is a mere 23 kilometres as the crow flies, the

Liffey meanders for a total length of around 135 kilometres. At the Poulaphouca Reservoir it is joined by its
first major tributary, the King's River. It then continues
westward towards Ballymore Eustace and Kilcullen, before
bending north, then north-east across the Liffey plain in
County Kildare, past Athgarvan, Newbridge, Clane,
Straffan and Celbridge. At Leixlip it is joined by another
major tributary, the Rye Water; also in Leixlip, a major
wastewater-treatment plant discharges into the river. Now
flowing eastward, the river enters County Dublin and
passes through Lucan, under the valley-spanning road
bridge for the M50 motorway, past the rowing clubs built
on its south banks to the weir at Islandbridge; here, the
Liffey becomes tidal. From Islandbridge it flows a further
four or five kilometres through the city before merging
into Dublin Bay. The two reservoirs and three hydroelec-
tric dams along its course help to control the river's
flow – during periods of heavy rain, water can be released
from the dams and reservoirs at a slower rate, thus reducing the likelihood of flooding downstream.

According to J. W. de Courcy's *The Liffey in Dublin*, it's
difficult to ascertain the exact origins of the river's name.
The *Annals of the Four Masters*, chronicles of medieval
Irish history that were compiled in the seventeenth century, record that the king of Ireland in the year 268 was
Cairbre Liffeachair, and it has been suggested that he
was named in this way because he grew up close to the
river. Later in the first millennium, the area of County
Kildare that lies within the loop of the river became

known as Airthear-Liffe. Numerous variations of the name have been recorded: Abhainn Liphthe, Avenlif, Avenesliz, Avon Liffey and Anna Liffey. The last form of the name is the one James Joyce drew on for Anna Livia Plurabelle in *Finnegans Wake*.

Prior to the building of the first Liffey bridge, Dublin consisted of a scattering of settlements along the north and south banks of the river. Travel between the two banks was either by fords – places where the river could be waded across – or by boat. The banks of the river tapered down to the water, and the river's navigability was limited by mud, sand and silt. The choice by the Vikings of the black pool of the Poddle as their harbour was an indication of the unsuitability of the Liffey's banks for tethering ships.

The first Liffey bridge was built in the eleventh century, just upstream from what is now the site of the Four Courts. Dubhgaill's bridge was constructed from timber and replaced the 'ford of hurdles' – hurdles were wattled frames woven from twigs which, laid across the river, could well have served as a primitive bridge – that had given Dublin its Irish-language name (Baile Átha Cliath, meaning 'town of the hurdled ford'). Dubhgaill's wooden bridge was swept away in around 1380 and replaced with a ferry service until the construction in 1428 of a masonry bridge, which was lined with shops – including a chapel, a bake-house and an inn – and known as the Bridge of Dublin, or the Old Bridge.

Between 1816 and 1818, the Bridge of Dublin was

replaced with a three-span masonry bridge – now known
as the Father Mathew Bridge, the second-oldest surviving bridge along the Liffey in Dublin. A breach in the
quay wall was made in advance of the bridge's installa-
tion; in March 1816, a man fell through the gap into the
river and died.

Walking along Victoria Quay on the south bank, I saw,
just across from the gates of the Guinness brewery, a
faded poster in a yellow-framed display case attached to
a lamp post. On closer inspection, it turned out to be an
old timetable from a defunct coach service that used to
run overnight between Dublin and Antwerp, also calling
at Manchester, Leeds, Nottingham, Birmingham and
London. The bus travelled three times a week in either
direction, a journey of nineteen hours. Checking later
online, I could see that, although the Irish route no longer
ran, the company, Ecolines, was still going strong, and
that from Antwerp there were connections to numerous
destinations in Poland, Ukraine and Russia. Perhaps the
removal of the Irish route was a sign that migrants were
going elsewhere?

The wall of the Guinness brewery runs the entire length
of Victoria Quay; from 1873 until 1961 the company
used a purpose-built jetty here to load its barges. A photo
taken in 1955 shows a narrow-gauge steam locomotive –
Guinness had its own railway system – pulling wagons
laden with wooden barrels along the jetty while a barge
waits for its load. Although there is a widespread belief

that Guinness stout used to be made with water from the Liffey, this was never the case. From its beginnings in 1759, the brewery drew water from the City Watercourse, the water supply diverted from the River Poddle, which passed through its site at St James's Gate; it now uses Dublin's public water supply.

I zigzagged across the three bridges that are clustered together linking Usher's Island (not an island at all, but the name of the south quay) to Ellis Quay. Rory O'More Bridge, an iron arch, painted light blue, was opened in 1861; it was first crossed by Queen Victoria and Prince Albert. A few metres downstream is the James Joyce Bridge, a lightweight single-span construction designed by the Spanish architect Santiago Calatrava and sustained by two angled arches that resemble eyelids. Frosted-glass platforms extend from the walkway; at night, these panels are illuminated from below, impressively. Minimalist stone benches extend along each walkway, and I sat down on one, facing west. The sleekness of the bridge was undermined somewhat, I thought, by Dublin City Council's decision to place a heavy iron bin, painted black and gold, at the end of the bench. At the same time, I found it reassuring: Dublin's character had been altered by the arrival of new buildings, flashy bridges and a newfound obsession with tech, but the council will still stick a bin wherever it wants. On the south side of the river is the four-storey red-brick Georgian town-house at Usher's Island where Joyce set his short story 'The Dead'. Painted in the window above the door are the words 'James Joyce House' and, below that, 'The Dead', as though the house were a labelled exhibit in a living museum.

Walking along Usher's Island gave me a view downstream that seemed somehow out of time. The sun slanted on to the river from the south-east, throwing shadows from the south quays, and in the morning haze the modern buildings seemed to dematerialize; suddenly, I felt I had a sense of how the city might have looked in the nineteenth century. The quayside four-storey red-brick houses seemed to lean on each other for support. At the centre of the vista was the Mellows Bridge, a three-arch stone bridge with white-painted balustrades, and the oldest bridge that I would encounter on my walk – it was built in 1764.

Crossing it, I heard the chirping of a songbird. On the bridge's footpath I saw, written in white paint, a graffito reading 'Troll Below'. When I reached Arran Quay I leaned against the quay wall and looked until I spotted a small finch scrabbling awkwardly on an east-facing niche. Stretching down the quay wall below me was a narrow stone stair leading to the river. All I had to do to reach the water was to climb over the wall and follow the steps to the bottom. A railing ran halfway down the outer edge so that the lower half of the stone staircase was exposed on the river side – to allow access to boats, I supposed. Standing on the quay, I looked down to the slimy lower steps and wondered what would happen if I lost my footing. I didn't jump the wall and I didn't descend the staircase.

Low tide was due at 9.16 a.m. I looked at my watch: it

was now 9.11. I hesitated, thought again about climbing down to the river, but instead continued walking downstream, passing a stationary queue of traffic that had formed along Arran Quay.

With the Four Courts looming immediately ahead, I crossed south via the Father Mathew Bridge and continued downriver along Merchant's Quay, past the Church of the Immaculate Conception, known as Adam and Eve's after the tavern in which the Franciscan monks secretly held Masses. The church is referenced in the watery first line of Joyce's *Finnegans Wake*: 'riverrun, past Eve and Adam's, from swerve of shore to bend of bay'. I crossed to Ormond Quay via O'Donovan Rossa Bridge; from here, I had a good view of Wood Quay on the south bank, and the headquarters of Dublin City Council: massive modernist concrete office blocks that were, controversially, built on the site of a Viking settlement. Continuing along Ormond Quay, I passed the old Ormond Hotel, which opened in 1889 but had been closed since 2006. The four-storey hotel was the setting for the 'Sirens' episode of Joyce's *Ulysses*. In February 2014, the council rejected a proposal from its owners to demolish the building and replace it with a six-storey hotel. At Capel Street, I crossed south to Wellington Quay. From Grattan Bridge – with its green-painted, wrought-iron latticework parapet and lamps decorated with seahorses – I could see the dome of City Hall; turning to my right, I saw that the dome's green patina was matched by that of the dome of the Four Courts.

On Wellington Quay, I paused over the arch where the Poddle joins the Liffey. The next crossing was the Millennium footbridge. Rather than continue to follow the footpath along Bachelor's Walk, I walked through a gap in the quay wall and on to the boardwalk, which dates from 1997. It runs along four north-bank quay walls for a total distance of some six hundred metres, but it is not continuous: at each bridge, you have to rejoin the regular path along the quay, traverse the road or footway carried by the bridge and then get back on the boardwalk. Although the boardwalk was conceived as a way of helping to bring the city closer to the river, the old infrastructure of the bridges seems to stand as a reminder that the river is something to be crossed, not engaged with.

The Ha'penny Bridge, a picturesque humpbacked iron footbridge that is perhaps the single most reproduced image of the city, was opened in 1816 as a toll bridge – the halfpenny charged to pedestrians was identical to the fee charged by the ferries that had previously plied the same crossing.

When I was child, the buses we took from the city centre in the direction of our home left from the south quays, not far from the Ha'penny Bridge. In the 1980s, I remember the bridge as being in poor condition – the wooden planks beneath the pathway were exposed, the surface tar worn away. I can recall the horror I felt when I looked between the planks to the water below – a sense of vertiginous fear I still experience when walking along seaside piers.

*

Aston Quay brought me to O'Connell Bridge, where I paused next to a stone stairway leading to the river at the southern side of the bridge. Could I climb down here? The stairway seemed worryingly narrow and greasy, as did its counterpart on the north quay, though there was a handrail running along the wall most of the way down. I looked at the river's surface, which lay low. I wondered whether I'd find a more suitable point to descend to the Liffey.

As I crossed O'Connell Bridge, I thought about something that had happened there a couple of years before. In July 2011, a homeless man, John Byrne, had been sitting on the bridge with his two pets, a dog and a rabbit. A young man, passing by, grabbed the rabbit by the ears and threw it into the river. Byrne – who was thirty-seven and had been living on the streets of Dublin since he was fifteen – jumped in after the rabbit. 'I was scared,' he told a reporter. 'Wouldn't anybody, going into freezing-cold water?' Once in the river, he retrieved the animal and swam to the northern pier of the bridge, on which he stood, holding the rabbit tight to his chest. With a crowd of onlookers watching, a fireman lowered a life-saver ring to Byrne, and he held it close to him, along with the rabbit. Soon a rescue boat arrived, bringing Byrne to the set of steps on the north quay. A few months later, the man who had thrown the rabbit into the river was convicted of animal cruelty and torture and sentenced to four months in prison.

Construction works for the Rosie Hackett Bridge

made it impossible to walk along the riverside footpath on Eden Quay – the whole riverside was fenced off. As I passed, I could see that the rails for the Luas – whose green line will cross the river here, creating the first linkage between the two lines – were being laid, and that the bridge was almost complete. At Butt Bridge, which carries four lanes of northbound traffic, I crossed to the south quay. I was now in the shadow of the Loop Line railway bridge – the one bridge downriver of Heuston station that I would not be able to cross. Directly below the Loop Line Bridge, I reached the top of a set of steps that led down to the river. This stairway, being broader than the others I'd considered, seemed more inviting, less hazardous. A set of railings followed the edge of the jutting quay, and had a gap to allow access to the steps; but against them a bearded man, who appeared to be homeless, sat.

I had a feeling that I wouldn't get a better chance than this. Perhaps the presence of the man near the steps steeled my nerves. Maybe at the back of my mind was the thought that, if things went badly and I fell in, I could shout and the man might hear me. I walked up to the man, who was bundled up in several layers of clothing and wore a woolly hat. I told him that I needed to get past him to get to the steps. He grunted in assent, moved aside and I passed through the gate. Perhaps because I had set reaching the Liffey as my aim, the next few moments assumed an almost dream-like level of unreality. I can't pretend that, as a lapsed Catholic, I wasn't alive to the symbolism of passing through a gate guarded by a bearded figure.

I slowly made my way down the granite steps. As I descended, I turned sideways, towards the quay wall, and eased down each stair in this way, thinking that it would somehow help my balance. The lower steps, which spent most of their time below water, were covered with a carpet of brown-green algae which squelched under my feet. I reached out to the quay wall for balance – it, too, was covered in algae, which left a slimy brown residue on my hand.

I was near the bottom step, upon which mussels had fixed themselves: their blue-black shells were pocked with the shells of even smaller bivalves. On the north bank, beyond the heavy pillars of the Loop Line Bridge, the Custom House sat bright in the morning sun. Directly above me, pedestrians crossed the Butt Bridge, oblivious of my presence. The surface of the river looked glassy, as if I could skate across it.

I reached the second-last step. A flotilla of trash – an empty wine bottle, a plastic bottle, a carrier bag and various sticks – bobbed in a stretch of dead water just off the bottom step. I had been considering for some time what I would do if I was able to make physical contact with the Liffey's water, and one image kept returning to me: on our walk through the Poddle tunnel, Dave Greene had reached down into that river's flow and allowed the water to trickle through his fingers.

Angling my satchel behind my back for balance, I

crouched and swept my right hand through the river's water. The cloudy water slipped through my fingers and trickled on to the steps next to my feet.

Above me I could hear the life of the city. Down here, by the river, I felt suddenly calmed. My fear of water was still powerful, but I hadn't fallen in. I withdrew from the edge of the stair and ascended slowly, passing through the gate.

The bearded man was no longer there, but I met him a bit further on and asked him his name: Constantino. He was from Romania. He had been holding a cardboard coffee cup and walking along the queue of traffic, asking for money. A few days later, I saw him with fellow Romanians on O'Connell Street, waiting for a bus.

In my enraptured state, I had to remind myself to stick to my rule of crossing at each bridge I encountered. I strolled over the Talbot Memorial Bridge and sat on a bench in front of the Custom House. As I sat, I watched a man wait for the traffic to stop at the lights before spraying a yellow liquid on car windscreens and polishing them with a cloth in the hope of payment. After a while sitting in the sun, I stood and walked east along the north quays, past the Famine memorial statues at Custom House Quay, and arrived at the Dublin Docklands Development Authority headquarters. Posted in the window were a couple of Section 25 listings, planning applications for a change of use to existing buildings. I had expected the DDDA to be gone by the time I returned to the city, but still it limped on.

I traversed the Seán O'Casey footbridge and turned left along City Quay. Having passed a couple of buildings, I reached the control room for the Samuel Beckett Bridge, which had a plastic jug kettle sitting on the counter. I crossed the bridge and expected to continue my journey, as I'd planned, along the North Wall Quay, past the Convention Centre and the empty Anglo Irish Bank building. The Beckett Bridge resembles a harp fallen on its edge. Thirty-one cable stays extend from an arc-shaped spar that curves skywards from its southern end and concludes in the air halfway across; each cable is tethered to the bridge's deck. The bridge can rotate ninety degrees to allow river traffic to pass through. Beyond the bridge on the north quay is the Convention Centre with its tilted cylindrical glass atrium resembling nothing so much as a colossal Guinness barrel hurled by a mythical giant into the façade of a provincial dancehall.

Instead, I saw that the quay was blocked off by police. A few protestors stood against barriers, facing towards the traffic that was being redirected away from the closed quay. They had various agendas. An anti-fracking group talked to passers-by, while a thin man who closely resembled the broadcaster Ryan Tubridy held an Irish tricolour that bore an anti-EU message. I asked him what was going on in the Convention Centre, and he told me that it was a meeting of the European People's Party – the pan-EU grouping of Christian Democrat parties – hosted by the Taoiseach and Fine Gael leader, Enda Kenny. Delegates, some pulling suitcases behind them, showed their ID passes to police as they passed through the barriers towards the glass Convention Centre. (When I had finished the walk and returned to my parents' house, I read some online news stories about the conference: protests held outside the centre the night before had turned violent. A little while after I walked away from the venue, Bono arrived to address the audience of centre-right politicians. 'Capitalism is a great thing,' he told the delegates. 'I should know.' Regardless of the content of the conference, the message was clear: Ireland was bouncing back.)

The security cordon meant that I couldn't progress further along the quay towards the seventeenth and final bridge, the East Link. So I turned back to the south side and walked along Sir John Rogerson's Quay. Looking across the river, I saw the PricewaterhouseCoopers headquarters next to the Convention Centre, and thought about the place of tax avoidance in Ireland's economy. Beyond the PwC offices was the still-unfinished Anglo Irish Bank building, its concrete skeleton open to the elements. I walked towards the possible future site of the U2 Tower, past the State Street office block and a white truck belonging to the Garda Water Unit Diving Section – perhaps they had been scoping the Liffey for possible threats to the event. Employees smoked outside the State Street building, a glass box that adjoined the hoardings that surrounded the U2 Tower site. Near the corner of the hoarding, someone had been smashing glass bottles. I could have continued on to the East Link, but it would have been a circuitous journey: the Grand Canal and the

River Dodder empty into the Liffey between Sir John Rogerson's Quay and Ringsend, and to get across those bodies of water I'd have had to veer significantly inland, away from the Liffey. My walk was complete, and I turned for home.

I passed the indifferent Facebook headquarters, then the old U2 studios on Hanover Quay. A lone black Labrador walked ahead of me. The sight made me realize that it had been a long time since I'd seen stray dogs wandering freely around the city. This dog, in particular, looked as though he were merely out for a stroll, like an old man taking the air on a spring morning. When he paused to urinate against the grey-painted pillar of a modern block – beneath the glass balconies of minimalist apartments and beside an appointment-only contemporary-furniture showroom – it seemed to me as if Old Dublin was passing judgement on the New.

Acknowledgements

To Laura O'Brien, for her love and support. To my parents, Tom and May Whitney, and my brother, Warren Whitney, for their reassurance and encouragement during the course of the book and throughout the years.

Thanks to Eamonn Hoban-Shelley, Jonathan O'Malley, Neil Carlin, Eugene Brennan, Joe Kennedy, Tony, Briege and Cathy O'Brien, Una Newell, Greg Baxter, Susan Tomaselli, Douglas Smith and Dave Power; and to all at the UCD Humanities Institute, South Dublin Libraries, Creative Cohesion in Sunderland and Mediaworks in Gateshead. Thanks also to Sarah Bannan at the Arts Council of Ireland.

I'd like to thank those who answered my queries and those who guided me around their patch of Dublin: Franc Myles, Alan Vickers, Michael Kenny, Robert Buckle, Dave Greene, Ursula Graham, Marian Bentley, Lorcan O'Toole, Tomás Maher, Ruadhán Mac Cormaic, Gerry Curran, Nicola Donnelly, Clodagh Sheehy, Graham Usher, Professor Declan Kiberd, Maeve O'Sullivan, Ben Kealy, Joe McCarthy, Valerie Jennings, Dr Niamh Moore-Cherry, Loretta Lambkin, Michael Phillips, Dr John Bartlett, Dr Karl McDonald, Peter O'Reilly, Dr Mary Gilmartin, Nuala Kane, Dr Thomas Kador, Tom Dowling, John F.

O'Connor, Fergal McCarthy, and Pat Yeates at the ESB Archive.

To Penguin Ireland, especially to my editor, Brendan Barrington, for his editorial guidance and for being such an enthusiastic supporter of this book from the beginning. And to Sarah Day, for her careful copy-editing.

The writing of *Hidden City* was made possible through the financial assistance of the Arts Council of Ireland, the Arts Office at South Dublin County Council and the John Heygate Award from the Authors' Foundation of the Society of Authors.